W9-ABS-322

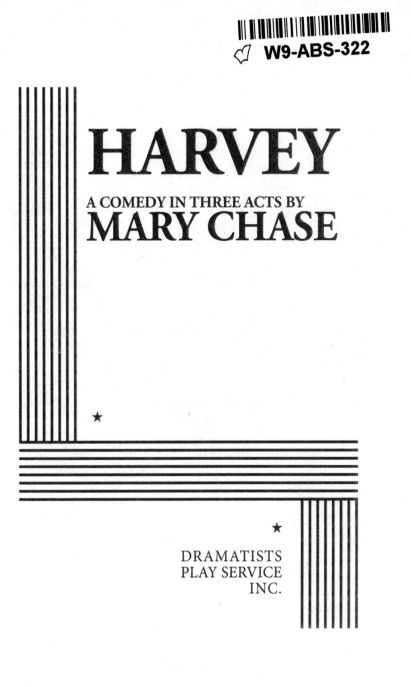

HARVEY

A COMEDY IN THREE ACTS BY
MARY CHASE

★

★

DRAMATISTS
PLAY SERVICE
INC.

HARVEY
Copyright © Renewed 1977, Mary Chase
Copyright © 1950, Mary Chase

Copyright © Renewed 1970, Mary Chase
Copyright © 1944, Mary Chase
under the title *The White Rabbit*

All Rights Reserved

CAUTION: Professionals and amateurs are hereby warned that performance of HARVEY is subject to payment of a royalty. It is fully protected under the copyright laws of the United States of America, and of all countries covered by the International Copyright Union (including the Dominion of Canada and the rest of the British Commonwealth), and of all countries covered by the Pan-American Copyright Convention, the Universal Copyright Convention, the Berne Convention, and of all countries with which the United States has reciprocal copyright relations. All rights, including without limitation professional/amateur stage rights, motion picture, recitation, lecturing, public reading, radio broadcasting, television, video or sound recording, all other forms of mechanical, electronic and digital reproduction, transmission and distribution, such as CD, DVD, the Internet, private and file-sharing networks, information storage and retrieval systems, photocopying, and the rights of translation into foreign languages are strictly reserved. Particular emphasis is placed upon the matter of readings, permission for which must be secured from the Author's agent in writing.

The English language stock and amateur stage performance rights in the United States, its territories, possessions and Canada for HARVEY are controlled exclusively by Dramatists Play Service, Inc., 440 Park Avenue South, New York, NY 10016. No professional or nonprofessional performance of the Play may be given without obtaining in advance the written permission of Dramatists Play Service, Inc., and paying the requisite fee.

Inquiries concerning all other rights should be addressed to Robert A. Freedman Dramatic Agency, Inc., 1501 Broadway, Suite 2310, New York, NY 10036.

SPECIAL NOTE

Anyone receiving permission to produce HARVEY is required to give credit to the Author as sole and exclusive Author of the Play on the title page of all programs distributed in connection with performances of the Play and in all instances in which the title of the Play appears, including printed or digital materials for advertising, publicizing or otherwise exploiting the Play and/or a production thereof. The name of the Author must appear on a separate line, in which no other name appears, immediately beneath the title and in size of type equal to 50% of the size of the largest, most prominent letter used for the title of the Play. No person, firm or entity may receive credit larger or more prominent than that accorded the Author.

SPECIAL NOTE ON SONGS AND RECORDINGS

Dramatists Play Service, Inc. neither holds the rights to nor grants permission to use any songs or recordings mentioned in the Play. Permission for performances of copyrighted songs, arrangements or recordings mentioned in this Play is not included in our license agreement. The permission of the copyright owner(s) must be obtained for any such use. For any songs and/or recordings mentioned in the Play, other songs, arrangements, or recordings may be substituted provided permission from the copyright owner(s) of such songs, arrangements or recordings is obtained; or songs, arrangements or recordings in the public domain may be substituted.

HARVEY was produced by Brock Pemberton at the Forty-Eighth Street Theatre, New York City, on November 1, 1944. It was directed by Antoinette Perry, with settings by John Root.

The cast was as follows:

MYRTLE MAE SIMMONS .... Jane Van Duser
VETA LOUISE SIMMONS .... Josephine Hull
ELWOOD P. DOWD .... Frank Fay
MISS JOHNSON .... Eloise Sheldon
MRS. ETHEL CHAUVENET .... Frederica Going
RUTH KELLY, R.N. .... Janet Tyler
DUANE WILSON .... Jesse White
LYMAN SANDERSON, M.D. .... Tom Seidel
WILLIAM R. CHUMLEY, M.D. .... Fred Irving Lewis
BETTY CHUMLEY .... Dora Clement
JUDGE OMAR GAFFNEY .... John Kirk
E. J. LOFGREN .... Robert Gist

SCENE SYNOPSIS

The action of the play takes place in a city in the Far West in the library of the old Dowd family mansion and the reception room of Chumley's Rest.

Time: The Present.

ACT I

Scene 1: The library, late afternoon.
Scene 2: Chumley's Rest, an hour later.

ACT II

Scene 1: The library, an hour later.
Scene 2: Chumley's Rest, four hours later.

ACT III

Chumley's Rest, a few minutes later.

HARVEY

ACT I

Scene 1

TIME: *Mid-afternoon of a spring day. The present.*

SCENE: *The library of the old Dowd family mansion— a room lined with books and set with heavy, old-fashioned furniture of a faded grandeur. The most conspicuous item in the room is an oil painting over a black marble Victorian mantelpiece at the lower part of the wall at stage* L. *This is the portrait of a lantern-jawed older woman. There are double doors at* R. *These doors now pulled apart, lead to the hallway and across to the parlor, which is not seen. Telephone is on small table* L. *This afternoon there is a festive look to the room—silver bowls with spring flowers set about. From the parlor* R. *comes the sound of a bad female voice singing, "I'm Called Little Buttercup."*

AT RISE: MYRTLE MAE *is discovered coming through door* R. *and as telephone rings, she goes to it.*

MYRTLE. Mrs. Simmons? Mrs. Simmons is my mother, but she has guests this afternoon. Who wants her? (*Respectful change in tone after she hears who it is.*) Oh—wait just a minute. Hang on just a minute. (*Goes to doorway* R. *and calls.*) Psst— Mother! (*Cranes her neck more.*) Psst—Mother! (*Crooks her finger insistently several times. Singing continues.*)
VETA. (*Enters* R., *humming "Buttercup."*) Yes, dear?
MYRTLE. Telephone.
VETA. (*Turning to go out again.*) Oh, no, dear. Not with all of them in there. Say I'm busy.
MYRTLE. But, Mother. It's the Society Editor of the Evening News Bee—

1

VETA. (*Turning.*) Oh—the Society Editor. She's very important. (*She fixes her hair and goes to phone. Her voice is very sweet. She throws out chest and assumes dignified pose.*) Good afternoon, Miss Ellerbe. This is Veta Simmons. Yes—a tea and reception for the members of the Wednesday Forum. You might say—program tea. My mother, you know—(*Waves hand toward portrait.*) the late Marcella Pinney Dowd, pioneer cultural leader she came here by ox-team as a child and she founded the Wednesday Forum. (MYRTLE *is watching out door.*) Myrtle—how many would you say?

MYRTLE. Seventy-five, at least. Say a hundred.

VETA. (*On phone.*) Seventy-five. Miss Tewksbury is the soloist, accompanied by Wilda McCurdy, accompanist.

MYRTLE. Come on! Miss Tewksbury is almost finished with her number.

VETA. She'll do an encore.

MYRTLE. What if they don't give her a lot of applause?

VETA. I've known her for years. She'll do an encore. (MYRTLE *again starts to leave.*) You might say that I am entertaining, assisted by my daughter, Miss Myrtle Mae Simmons. (*To Myrtle—indicates her dress.* MYRTLE MAE *crosses to* C.) What color would you call that?

MYRTLE. Rancho Rose, they told me.

VETA. (*Into phone.*) Miss Myrtle Mae Simmons looked charming in a modish Rancho Rose toned crepe, picked up at the girdle with a touch of magenta on emerald. I wish you could see her, Miss Ellerbe.

MYRTLE. (*Crossing up* R. *Looks through door.*) Mother— please—she's almost finished and where's the cateress?

VETA. (*To Myrtle.*) Everything's ready. The minute she's finished singing we open the dining-room doors and we begin pouring. (*Into phone.*) The parlors and halls are festooned with smilax. Yes, festooned. (*Makes motion in air with finger.*) That's right. Yes, Miss Ellerbe, this is the first party we've had in years. There's a reason but I don't want it in the papers. We all have our troubles, Miss Ellerbe. The guest list? Oh, yes—

MYRTLE. Mother—come.

VETA. If you'll excuse me now, Miss Ellerbe. I'll call you later. (*Hangs up.*)

MYRTLE. Mother—Mrs. Chauvenet just came in!

2

VETA. *(Arranging flowers on phone table.)* Mrs. Eugene Chauvenet Senior! Her father was a scout with Buffalo Bill.

MYRTLE. So that's where she got that hat!

VETA. *(As she and* MYRTLE *start to exit.)* Myrtle, you must be nice to Mrs. Chauvenet. She has a grandson about your age.

MYRTLE. But what difference will it make, with Uncle Elwood?

VETA. Myrtle Mae—remember! We agreed not to talk about that this afternoon. The point of this whole party is to get you started. We work through those older women to the younger group.

MYRTLE. We can't have anyone here in the evenings, and that's when men come to see you—in the evenings. The only reason we can even have a party this afternoon is because Uncle Elwood is playing pinochle at the Fourth Avenue Firehouse. Thank God for the firehouse!

VETA. I know—but they'll just have to invite you out and it won't hurt them one bit. Oh, Myrtle—you've got so much to offer. I don't care what anyone says, there's something sweet about every young girl. And a man takes that sweetness, and look what he does with it! *(Crosses to mantel with flowers.)* But you've got to meet somebody, Myrtle. That's all there is to it.

MYRTLE. If I do they say, That's Myrtle Mae Simmons! Her uncle is Elwood P. Dowd—the biggest screwball in town. Elwood P. Dowd and his pal—

VETA. *(Puts hand on her mouth.)* You promised.

MYRTLE. *(Crossing above table, sighs.)* All right—let's get them into the dining-room.

VETA. Now when the members come in here and you make your little welcome speech on behalf of your grandmother— be sure to do this. *(Gestures toward portrait on mantel.)*

MYRTLE. *(In fine disgust—business with flowers.)* And then after that, I mention my Uncle Elwood and say a few words about his pal Harvey. Damn Harvey! *(In front of table, as she squats.)*

VETA. *(The effect on her is electric. She runs over and closes doors. Crosses behind table to* C.*)* Myrtle Mae—that's right! Let everybody in the Wednesday Forum hear you. You said that name. You promised you wouldn't say that name and you said it.

3

MYRTLE. (*Rising, starting to cross* L.) I'm sorry, Mother. But how do you know Uncle Elwood won't come in and introduce Harvey to everybody? (*To mantel. Places flowers on it.*)

VETA. This is unkind of you, Myrtle Mae. Elwood is the biggest heartache I have. Even if people do call him peculiar he's still my brother, and he won't be home this afternoon.

MYRTLE. Are you sure?

VETA. Of course I'm sure.

MYRTLE. But Mother, why can't we live like other people?

VETA. Must I remind you again? Elwood is not living with us —we are living with him.

MYRTLE. Living with him and Harvey! Did Grandmother know about Harvey?

VETA. I've wondered and wondered about that. She never wrote me if she did.

MYRTLE. Why did she have to leave all her property to Uncle Elwood?

VETA. Well, I suppose it was because she died in his arms. People are sentimental about things like that.

MYRTLE. You always say that and it doesn't make sense. She couldn't make out her will after she died, could she?

VETA. Don't be didactic, Myrtle Mae. It's not becoming in a young girl, and men loathe it. Now don't forget to wave your hand.

MYRTLE. I'll do my best. (*Opens door.*)

VETA. Oh, dear—Miss Tewksbury's voice is certainly fading!

MYRTLE. But not fast enough. (*She exits.*)

VETA. (*Exits through door, clapping hands, pulling down girdle.*) Lovely, Miss Tewksbury—perfectly lovely. I loved it. (*Through door* U.L. *enters* ELWOOD P. DOWD. *He is a man about 47 years old with a dignified bearing, and yet a dreamy expression in his eyes. His expression is benign, yet serious to the point of gravity. He wears an overcoat and a battered old hat. This hat, reminiscent of the Joe College era, sits on the top of his head. Over his arm he carries another hat and coat. As he enters, although he is alone, he seems to be ushering and bowing someone else in with him. He bows the invisible person over to a chair. His step is light, his movements quiet and his voice low-pitched.*)

ELWOOD. (*To invisible person.*) Excuse me a moment. I have to answer the phone. Make yourself comfortable, Harvey. (*Phone rings.*) Hello. Oh, you've got the wrong number. But

4

how are you, anyway? This is Elwood P. Dowd speaking. I'll do? Well, thank you. And what is your name, my dear? Miss Elsie Greenawalt? *(To chair.)* Harvey, it's a Miss Elsie Greenawalt. How are you today, Miss Greenawalt? That's fine. Yes, my dear. I would be happy to join your club. I belong to several clubs now—the University Club, the Country Club and the Pinochle Club at the Fourth Avenue Firehouse. I spend a good deal of my time there, or at Charlie's Place, or over at Eddie's Bar. And what is your club, Miss Greenawalt? *(He listens—then turns to empty chair.)* Harvey, I get the Ladies Home Journal, Good Housekeeping and the Open Road for Boys for two years for six twenty-five. *(Back to phone.)* It sounds fine to me. I'll join it. *(To chair.)* How does it sound to you, Harvey? *(Back to phone.)* Harvey says it sounds fine to him also, Miss Greenawalt. He says he will join, too. Yes—two subscriptions. Mail everything to this address. . . . I hope I will have the pleasure of meeting you some time, my dear. Harvey, she says she would like to meet me. When? When would you like to meet me, Miss Greenawalt? Why not right now? My sister seems to be having a few friends in and we would consider it an honor if you would come and join us. My sister will be delighted. 343 Temple Drive—I hope to see you in a very few minutes. Goodbye, my dear. *(Hangs up.)* She's coming right over. *(Moves C. to* HARVEY.*)* Harvey, don't you think we'd better freshen up? Yes, so do I. *(He takes up hats and coats and exits* L.*)*

VETA. *(Enters, followed by* MAID.*)* I can't seem to remember where I put that guest list. I must read it to Miss Ellerbe . . . . Have you seen it, Miss Johnson?

MAID. No, I haven't, Mrs. Simmons.

VETA. Look on my dresser. (MAID *exits* L.)

MYRTLE. *(Enters* R.*)* Mother—Mrs. Chauvenet—she's asking for you. *(Turning—speaking in oh-so-sweet tone to someone in hall.)* Here's Mother, Mrs. Chauvenet. Here she is. *(Enter* MRS. CHAUVENET. *She is a woman of about 65—heavy, dressed with the casual sumptuousness of a wealthy Western society woman—in silvery gold and plush, and mink scarf even though it is a spring day. She rushes over to* VETA.*)*

MRS. CHAUVENET. Veta Louise Simmons! I thought you were dead. *(Gets to her and takes hold of her.)*

VETA. *(Rushing to her, they kiss.)* Aunt Ethel! *(Motioning to*

5

MYRTLE *to come forward and meet the great lady.*) Oh, no—
I'm very much alive—thank you—

MRS. CHAUVENET. (*Turning to* MYRTLE.)—and this full-grown
girl is your daughter—I've known you since you were a baby.

MYRTLE. I know.

MRS. CHAUVENET. What's your name, dear?

VETA. (*Proudly.*) This is Myrtle—Aunt Ethel. Myrtle Mae—
for the two sisters of her father. He's dead. That's what confused you.

MRS. CHAUVENET. Where's Elwood?

VETA. (*With a nervous glance at* MYRTLE MAE.) He couldn't
be here, Aunt Ethel—now let me get you some tea. (*Cross to*
R. *of table* R.)

MRS. CHAUVENET. Elwood isn't here?

VETA. No —

MRS. CHAUVENET. Oh, shame on him. That was the main reason I came. (*Takes off scarf—puts it on chair* L. *of table.*) I
want to see Elwood.

VETA. Come—there are loads of people anxious to speak to
you.

MRS. CHAUVENET. Do you realize, Veta, it's been years since
I've seen Elwood?

VETA. No—where does the time go?

MRS. CHAUVENET. But I don't understand it. I was saying to
Mr. Chauvenet only the other night—what on earth do you
suppose has happened to Elwood Dowd? He never comes to
the club dances any more. I haven't seen him at a horse
show in years. Does Elwood see anybody these days?

VETA. (*And* MYRTLE, *with a glance at each other.*) Oh, yes—
Aunt Ethel. Elwood sees somebody.

MYRTLE. Oh, yes.

MRS. CHAUVENET. (*To* MYRTLE.) Your Uncle Elwood, child, is
one of my favorite people. (VETA *rises and crosses around
chair* R. *of table.*) Always has been.

VETA. Yes, I remember.

MRS. CHAUVENET. Is Elwood happy, Veta?

VETA. Elwood's very happy, Aunt Ethel. You don't need to
worry about Elwood—— (*Looks through* R. *doorway. She is
anxious to get the subject on something else.*) Why, there's
Mrs. Frank Cummings—just came in. Don't you want to
speak to her?

MRS. CHAUVENET. (*Crosses above chair to peer out* R.) My--but she looks ghastly! Hasn't she failed though?

VETA. If you think she looks badly—you should see him!

MRS. CHAUVENET. Is that so? I must have them over. (*Looks again.*) She looks frightful. I thought she was dead.

VETA. Oh, no.

MRS. CHAUVENET. Now—what about tea, Veta?

VETA. Certainly —(*Starts forward to lead the way.*) If you will forgive me, I will precede you —— (ELWOOD *enters.* MRS. CHAUVENET *turns back to pick up her scarf from chair, and sees him.*)

MRS. CHAUVENET. (*Rushing forward.*) Elwood! Elwood Dowd! Bless your heart.

ELWOOD. (*Coming forward and bowing as he takes her hand.*) Aunt Ethel! What a pleasure to come in and find a beautiful woman waiting for me!

MRS. CHAUVENET. (*Looking at him fondly.*) Elwood—you haven't changed.

VETA. (*Moves forward quickly, takes hold of her.*) Come along, Aunt Ethel—you mustn't miss the party.

MYRTLE. There's punch if you don't like tea.

MRS. CHAUVENET. But I do like tea. Stop pulling at me, you two. Elwood, what night next week can you come to dinner?

ELWOOD. Any night. Any night at all, Aunt Ethel—I would be delighted.

VETA. Elwood, there's some mail for you today. I took it up to your room.

ELWOOD. Did you, Veta? That was nice of you. Aunt Ethel— I want you to meet Harvey. As you can see he's a Pooka. (*Turns toward air beside him.*) Harvey, you've heard me speak of Mrs. Chauvenet? We always called her Aunt Ethel. She is one of my oldest and dearest friends. (*Inclines head toward space and goes "Hmm!" and then listens as though not hearing first time. Nods as though having heard someone next to him speak.*) Yes—yes—that's right. She's the one. This is the one. (*To* MRS. CHAUVENET.) He says he would have known you anywhere. (*Then as a confused, bewildered look comes over* MRS. CHAUVENET'S *face and as she looks to* L. *and* R. *of* ELWOOD *and cranes her neck to see behind him—*ELWOOD *not seeing her expression, crosses her towards* VETA *and* MYRTLE MAE.) You both look lovely. (*Turns to the air next to him.*) Come on in with me, Harvey—We must say hello to all of our friends —— (*Bows to* MRS. CHAUVENET.) I beg your par-

7

don, Aunt Ethel. If you'll excuse me for one moment ——
(*Puts his hand gently on her arm, trying to turn her.*)
MRS. CHAUVENET. What?

ELWOOD. You are standing in his way —— (SHE *gives a little—
her eyes wide on him.*) Come along, Harvey. (HE *watches the
invisible Harvey cross to door, then stops him.*) Uh-uh! (EL-
WOOD *goes over to door. He turns and pantomimes as he ar-
ranges the tie and brushes off the head of the invisible Harvey. Then he does the same thing to his own tie. They are
ALL watching him,* MRS. CHAUVENET *in horrified fascination.
The heads of* VETA *and* MYRTLE, *bowed in agony.*) Go right
on in, Harvey. I'll join you in a minute. (*He pantomimes as
though slapping him on the back, and ushers him out. Then
turns and comes back to* MRS. CHAUVENET.) Aunt Ethel, I can
see you are disturbed about Harvey. Please don't be. He stares
like that at everybody. It's his way. But he liked you. I could
tell. He liked you very much. (*Pats her arm reassuringly,
smiles at her, then calmly and confidently goes on out at* R.
*After his exit—*MRS. CHAUVENET, MYRTLE *and* VETA *are silent.
Finally* VETA—*with a resigned tone—clears her throat.*)
VETA. (*Looking at* MRS. CHAUVENET.) Some tea—perhaps—?
MRS. CHAUVENET. Why, I—not right now—I—well—I think I'll
be running along. (*Crosses back of table.*)
MYRTLE. But ——
VETA. (*Putting a hand over hers to quiet her.*) I'm so sorry ——
MRS. CHAUVENET. I'll—I'll be talking to you soon. Goodbye –
goodbye —— (*She exits quickly out* L. VETA *stands stiffly—her
anger paralyzing her.* MYRTLE *finally tiptoes over and closes
one side of door—peeking over, but keeping herself out of
sight.*)
MYRTLE. Oh, God —— (*Starts to run for doorway.*) Oh, my
God!
VETA. Myrtle—where are you going?
MYRTLE. Up to my room. He's introducing Harvey to every-
body. I can't face those people now. I wish I were dead.
VETA. Come back here. Stay with me. We'll get him out of
there and upstairs to his room.
MYRTLE. I won't do it. I can't. I can't.
VETA. Myrtle Mae! (MYRTLE *stops.* VETA *goes over to her and
pulls her down* C., *where they are directly in line with door-
way.*) Now—pretend I'm fixing your corsage.
MYRTLE. (*Covering her face with her hands in shame.*) Oh,

8

Mother!

VETA. We've got to. Pretend we're having a gay little chat. Keep looking. When you catch his eye, tell me. He always comes when I call him. Now, then—do you see him yet?

MYRTLE. No—not yet. How do you do, Mrs. Cummings.

VETA. Smile, can't you? Have you no pride? I'm smiling —— (*Waves off* R. *and laughs.*) and he's my own brother!

MYRTLE. Oh, Mother—people get run over by trucks every day. Why can't something like that happen to Uncle Elwood?

VETA. Myrtle Mae Simmons, I'm ashamed of you. This thing is not your uncle's fault. (*Phone rings.*)

MYRTLE. Ouch! You're sticking me with that pin!

VETA. That's Miss Ellerbe. Keep looking. Keep smiling. (*She goes to phone.*)

MYRTLE. Mrs. Cummings is leaving. Uncle Elwood must have told her what Harvey is. Oh, God!

VETA. (*On phone.*) Hello—this is Mrs. Simmons. Should you come in the clothes you have on—What have you on? Who is this? But I don't know any Miss Greenawalt. Should you what?—May I ask who invited you? Mr. Dowd! Thank you just the same, but I believe there has been a mistake.—Well, I never!

MYRTLE. Never what?

VETA. One of your Uncle Elwood's friends. She asked me if she should bring a quart of gin to the Wednesday Forum!

MYRTLE. There he is—he's talking to Mrs. Halsey.

VETA. Is Harvey with him?

MYRTLE. What a thing to ask! How can I tell? How can anybody tell but Uncle Elwood?

VETA. (*Calls.*) Oh, Elwood, could I see you a moment, dear? (*To* Myrtle.) I promise you your Uncle Elwood has disgraced us for the last time in this house. I'm going to do something I've never done before.

MYRTLE. What did you mean just now when you said this was not Uncle Elwood's fault? If it's not his fault, whose fault is it?

VETA. Never you mind. I know whose fault it is. Now lift up your head and smile and go back in as though nothing had happened.

MYRTLE. You're no match for Uncle Elwood.

VETA. You'll see. (ELWOOD *is coming.*)

MYRTLE. (*As* THEY *pass at door.*) Mother's waiting for you.

(*She exits.*)

VETA. Elwood! Could I see you for a moment, dear?

ELWOOD. Yes, sister. Excuse me, Harvey. (VETA *steps quickly over and pulls double doors together.*)

VETA. Elwood, would you mind sitting down in here and waiting for me until the party is over? I wan't to talk to you. It's very important.

ELWOOD. (*Crossing* C.) Of course, sister. I happen to have a little free time right now and you're welcome to all of it, Veta. (*Business.*) Do you want Harvey to wait too?

VETA. (*To* R. *of* ELWOOD. *Quite seriously—not in a pampering, humoring tone at all.*) Yes, Elwood. I certainly do. (*She steals out—watching him as she crosses through* R. *door. After she has gone out we see doors being pulled together from the outside and hear the click of a lock.* ELWOOD *goes calmly over to bookcase, peruses it carefully, and then when he had found the book he wants, takes it out and from behind it pulls a half-filled pint bottle of liquor.*)

ELWOOD. (*Looking at book he holds in one hand.*) Ah—Jane Austen. (*He gets one chair, pulls it down, facing front. Gets chair* L. *and pulls it right alongside. Sits down, sets bottle on floor between chairs.*) Sit down, Harvey. Veta wants to talk to us. She said it was important. I think she wants to congratulate us on the impression we made at her party. (*Reads. Turns to Harvey. Inclines head and listens, then looks at back of book and answers as though Harvey had asked what edition it is, who published it and what are those names on the fly leaf; turning head toward empty chair each time and twice saying "Hmm?"*) Jane Austen—De Luxe Edition—Limited—Grosset and Dunlap—The usual acknowledgements. Chapter One ——

AND THE CURTAIN FALLS

ACT I

Scene 2

SCENE: *The office in the main building of Chumley's Rest—a sanitarium for mental patients. The wall at back*

10

is half plaster and half glass. There is a door U.C. *Through this we can see the corridor of the sanitarium itself. In the wall lower* R. *is a door which is lettered "Dr. Chumley." Above on* R. *wall is a bookcase, a small filing-case on top of it. Across the room at upper* L. *is another door lettered "Dr. Sanderson." Down* L. *is the door leading from the outside. There is a big desk* L.C. *at right-angles with footlights, with chair either side of desk. At* R. *is a table with chairs on either side. One small chair up-stage* C.

TIME: *An hour after the curtain of Scene 1.*

At rise MISS RUTH KELLY, *head nurse at Chumley's Rest, is seated* L. *of desk, taking notes as she talks to* VETA SIMMONS, *who stands* C. MISS KELLY *is a very pretty young woman of about twenty-four. She is wearing a starched white uniform and cap. As she talks to Veta she writes on a slip of paper with a pencil.*

KELLY. (*Writing.*) Mrs. O. R. Simmons, 343 Temple Drive, is that right?

VETA. (*Nodding, taking handkerchief from handbag.*) We were born and raised there. It's old but we love it. It's our home. (*Crosses to table* R., *puts down handbag.*)

KELLY. And you wish to enter your brother here at the sanitarium for treatment. Your brother's name?

VETA. (*Coming back to desk—raising handkerchief to eyes and dabbing.*) It's — oh ——

KELLY. Mrs. Simmons, what is your brother's name?

VETA. I'm sorry. Life is not easy for any of us. I'll have to hold my head up and go on just the same. That's what I keep telling Myrtle and that's what Myrtle Mae keeps telling me. She's heart-broken about her Uncle Elwood—Elwood P. Dowd. That's it. (*Sits chair* R. *of desk.*)

KELLY. (*Writing.*) Elwood P. Dowd. His age?

VETA. Forty-seven the 24th of last April. He's Taurus—Taurus —the bull. I'm Leo, and Myrtle is on a cusp.

KELLY. Forty-seven. Is he married?

VETA. No, Elwood has never married. He stayed with mother. He was always a great home boy. He loved his home.

KELLY. You have him with you now?

VETA. He's in a taxicab down in the driveway. KELLY rings

11

buzzer.) I gave the driver a dollar to watch him, but I didn't tell the man why. You can't tell these things to perfect strangers. (*Enter* WILSON, C. *He is the sanitarium strongarm. He is a big burly attendant, black-browed, about 28.* KELLY *crosses in front of desk toward bookcase.*)

KELLY. Mr. Wilson, would you step down to a taxi in the driveway and ask a Mr. Dowd if he would be good enough to step up to Room number 24—South Wing G?

WILSON. (*Glaring at* L. *upper corner of desk.*) Ask him?

KELLY. (*Above table* R., *with a warning glance toward Veta.*) This is his sister, Mrs. Simmons. (KELLY *crosses to cabinet* R. *for card.*)

WILSON. (*With a feeble grin.*) How do—why, certainly—be glad to *escort* him. (*Exits down* L.)

VETA. Thank you.

KELLY. (*Coming* C. *to* R. *of Veta—handing her printed slip.*) The rates here, Mrs. Simmons—you'll find them printed on this card.

VETA. (*Waving it away.*) That will all be taken care of by my mother's estate. The late Marcella Pinney Dowd. Judge Gaffney is our attorney.

KELLY. Now I'll see if Dr. Sanderson can see you. (*Starts toward office* L.)

VETA. Dr. Sanderson? I want to see Dr. Chumley himself.

KELLY. (*Backs down* C.) Oh, Mrs. Simmons, Dr. Sanderson is the one who sees everybody. Dr. Chumley sees no one.

VETA. He's still head of this institution, isn't he? He's still a psychiatrist, isn't he?

KELLY. (*Shocked at such heresy.*) Still a psychiatrist! Dr. Chumley is more than that. He is a psychiatrist with a national reputation. Whenever people have mental breakdowns they at once think of Dr. Chumley.

VETA. (*Pointing.*) That's his office, isn't it? Well, you march right in and tell him I want to see him. If he knows who's in here he'll come out here.

KELLY. I wouldn't dare disturb him, Mrs. Simmons. I would be discharged if I did.

VETA. Well, I don't like to be pushed off onto any second fiddle.

KELLY. Dr. Sanderson is nobody's second fiddle. (*Crosses to back of desk, her eyes aglow.*) He's young, of course, and he hasn't been out of medical school very long, but Dr. Chumley

tried out twelve and kept Dr. Sanderson. He's really wonderful—
(Catches herself.) to the patients.

VETA. Very well. Tell him I'm here.

KELLY. *(Straightens her cap. As she exits into door L., primps.)*
Right away.

VETA. *(She rises, takes off coat—puts it on back of chair R. of desk,
sighs.)* Oh dear—oh dear. *(And crosses to table R. WILSON and
ELWOOD appear in corridor. ELWOOD pulls over a little from WILSON
and sees VETA.)*

ELWOOD. Veta—isn't this wonderful—! *(WILSON takes him
forcefully off up-stairs. VETA is still jumpy and nervous from the surprise,
and her back to door U.L. as—enter DR. SANDERSON. LYMAN
SANDERSON is a good-looking young man of 27 or 28. He is wearing a
starched white coat over dark trousers. His eyes follow MISS KELLY, who
has walked out before him and gone out C., closing C. doors. Then he sees
VETA, pulls down his jacket and gets a professional bearing. VETA has
not heard him come in. She is still busy with the compact.)*

SANDERSON. *(Looking at slip in his hand. Crosses to C.)* Mrs.
Simmons?

VETA. *(Startled—she jumps.)* Oh—oh dear—I didn't hear you
come in. You startled me. You're Dr. Sanderson?

SANDERSON. *(He nods.)* Yes. Will you be seated, please?

VETA. *(Sits in chair L. of table R.)* Thank you. I hope you don't
think I'm jumpy like that all the time, but I—

SANDERSON. *(Crossing in front of table to chair R.)* Of course
not. Miss Kelly tells me you are concerned about your brother.
Dowd, is it? Elwood P. Dowd?

VETA. Yes, Doctor—he's—this isn't easy for me, Doctor.

SANDERSON. *(Kindly.)* Naturally these things aren't easy for
the families of patients. I understand.

VETA. *(Twisting her handkerchief nervously.)* It's what Elwood's
doing to himself, Doctor—that's the thing. Myrtle Mae has a
right *to* nice friends. She's young and her whole life is before
her. That's my daughter.

SANDERSON. *(Sits R. of table.)* Your daughter. How long has
it been since you began to notice any peculiarity in your
brother's actions?

VETA. I noticed it right away when Mother died, and Myrtle
Mae and I came back home from Des Moines to live with
Elwood. I could see that he—that he— *(Twists handkerchief—
looks pleadingly at SANDERSON.)*

SANDERSON. That he—what? Take your time, Mrs. Simmons.

Don't strain. Let it come. I'll wait for it.

VETA. Doctor—everything I say to you is confidential? Isn't it?

SANDERSON. That's understood.

VETA. Because it's a slap in the face to everything we've stood for in this community the way Elwood is acting now.

SANDERSON. I am not a gossip, Mrs. Simmons. I am a psychiatrist.

VETA. Well—for one thing—he drinks.

SANDERSON. To excess?

VETA. To excess? Well—don't you call it excess when a man never lets a day go by without stepping into one of those cheap taverns, sitting around with riffraff and people you never heard of? Inviting them to the house—playing cards with them—giving them food and money. And here I am trying to get Myrtle Mae started with a nice group of young people. If that isn't excess I'm sure I don't know what excess is.

SANDERSON. I didn't doubt your statement, Mrs. Simmons. I merely asked if your brother drinks.

VETA. Well, yes, I say definitely Elwood drinks and I want him committed out here permanently, because I cannot stand another day of that Harvey. Myrtle and I have to set a place at the table for Harvey. We have to move over on the sofa and make room for Harvey. We have to answer the telephone when Elwood calls and asks to speak to Harvey. Then at the party this afternoon with Mrs. Chauvenet there—We didn't even know anything about Harvey until we came back here. Doctor, don't you think it would have been a little bit kinder of Mother to have written and told me about Harvey? Be honest, now—don't you?

SANDERSON. I really couldn't answer that question, because I —

VETA. I can. Yes—it certainly would have.

SANDERSON. This person you call Harvey—who is he?

VETA. He's a rabbit.

SANDERSON. Perhaps—but just who is he? Some companion—someone your brother has picked up in these bars, of whom you disapprove?

VETA. (*Patiently.*) Doctor—I've been telling you. Harvey is a rabbit—a big white rabbit—six feet high—or is it six feet and a half? Heavens knows I ought to know. He's been around the house long enough.

14

SANDERSON. *(Regarding her narrowly.)* Now, Mrs. Simmons, let me understand this—you say—

VETA. *(Impatient.)* Doctor—do I have to keep repeating myself? My brother insists that his closest friend is this big white rabbit. This rabbit is named Harvey. Harvey lives at our house. Don't you understand? He and Elwood go every place together. Elwood buys railroad tickets, theater tickets, for both of them. As I told Myrtle Mae—if your uncle was so lonesome he had to bring something home—why couldn't he bring home something human? He has me, doesn't he? He has Myrtle Mae, doesn't he? *(She leans forward.)* Doctor—*(She rises to him.* HE *inclines toward her.)* I'm going to tell you something I've never told anybody in the world before. *(Puts her hand on his shoulder.)* Every once in a while I see that big white rabbit myself. Now isn't that terrible? I've never even told that to Myrtle Mae.

SANDERSON. *(Now convinced. Starts to rise.)* Mrs. Simmons—

VETA. *(Straightening.)* And what's more—he's every bit as big as Elwood says he is. Now don't ever tell that to anybody, Doctor. I'm ashamed of it. *(Crosses to c., to chair R. of desk.)*

SANDERSON. *(Crosses to VETA.)* I can see that you have been under a great nervous strain recently.

VETA. Well—I certainly have.

SANDERSON. Grief over your mother's death depressed you considerably?

VETA. *(Sits chair R. of desk.)* Nobody knows how much.

SANDERSON. Been losing sleep?

VETA. How could anybody sleep with that going on?

SANDERSON. *(Crosses to back of desk.)* Short-tempered over trifles?

VETA. You just try living with those two and see how your temper holds up.

SANDERSON. *(Presses buzzer.)* Loss of appetite?

VETA. No one could eat at a table with my brother and a big white rabbit. Well, I'm finished with it. I'll sell the house—be appointed conservator of Elwood's estate, and Myrtle Mae and I will be able to entertain our friends in peace. It's too much, Doctor. I just can't stand it.

SANDERSON. *(Has been repeatedly pressing a buzzer on his desk. He looks with annoyance toward hall door. His answer now to* VETA *is gentle.)* Of course, Mrs. Simmons. Of course it is. You're tired.

VETA. *(She nods.)* Oh, yes I am.

SANDERSON. You've been worrying a great deal.

VETA. *(Nods.)* Yes, I have. I can't help it.

SANDERSON. And now I'm going to help you.

VETA. Oh, Doctor...

SANDERSON. *(Goes cautiously to door—watching her.)* Just sit there quietly, Mrs. Simmons. I'll be right back. *(He exits C.)*

VETA. *(Sighing with relief, rises and calls out as she takes coat.)* I'll just go down to the cab and get Elwood's things. *(She exits out down L. SANDERSON, KELLY and WILSON come from C.)*

SANDERSON. Why didn't someone answer the buzzer?

KELLY. I didn't hear you, Doctor—

SANDERSON. I rang and rang. *(Looks into his office. It is empty.)* Mrs. Simmons— *(Looks out door L., shuts it, comes back.)* Sound the gong, Wilson. That poor woman must not leave the grounds.

WILSON. She's made with a getaway, huh, doc? *(WILSON presses a button on the wall and we hear a loud gong sounding.)*

SANDERSON. Her condition is serious. Go after her. *(WILSON exits C.)*

KELLY. I can't believe it. *(Above a chair R. of desk. SANDERSON sits L. of desk and picks up phone.)*

SANDERSON. Main gate. Henry, Dr. Sanderson. Allow no one out of the main gate. We're looking for a patient. *(Hangs up.)* I shouldn't have left her alone, but no one answered the buzzer.

KELLY. Wilson was in South, Doctor.

SANDERSON. *(Making out papers.)* What have we available, Miss Kelly?

KELLY. Number 13, upper West R., is ready, Doctor.

SANDERSON. Have her taken there immediately, and I will prescribe preliminary treatment. I must contact her brother. Dowd is the name. Elwood P. Dowd. Get him on the telephone for me, will you please, Miss Kelly?

KELLY. But Doctor—I didn't know it was the woman who needed the treatment. She said it was for her brother.

SANDERSON. Of course she did. It's the oldest dodge in the world—always used by a cunning type of psychopath. She apparently knew her brother was about to commit her, so she came out to discredit him. Get him on the telephone, please.

KELLY. But, Doctor—I thought the woman was all right, so I had Wilson take the brother up to No. 24 South Wing G. He's there now.

SANDERSON. (*Staring at her with horror.*) You had Wilson take the brother in? No gags, please Kelly. You're not serious, are you?

KELLY. Oh, I did, Doctor. I did. Oh, Doctor, I'm terribly sorry.

SANDERSON. Oh, well then, if you're sorry, that fixes everything. (*He starts to pick up house phone and finishes the curse under his breath.*) Oh — no! (*Buries his head in his hands.*)

KELLY. I'll do it, Doctor. I'll do it. (*She takes phone.*) Miss Dunphy—will you please unlock the door to Number 24—and give Mr. Dowd his clothes and ——? (*Looks at Sanderson for direction.*)

SANDERSON. Ask him to step down to the office right away.

KELLY. (*Into phone.*) Ask him to step down to the office right away. There's been a terrible mistake and Dr. Sanderson wants to explain—

SANDERSON. (*Crosses below table to* C.) Explain? Apologize!

KELLY. (*Hanging up.*) Thank heaven they hadn't put him in a hydro tub yet. She'll let him out.

SANDERSON. (*Staring at her.*) Beautiful—and dumb, too. It's almost too good to be true.

KELLY. (*Crosses to* L. *of Sanderson.*) Doctor—I feel terrible. I didn't know. Judge Gaffney called and said Mrs. Simmons' and her brother would be out here, and when she came in here—you don't have to be sarcastic.

SANDERSON. Oh, don't I? Stop worrying. We'll squirm out of it some way. (*Thinking—starts toward* R.)

KELLY. Where are you going?

SANDERSON. I've got to tell the chief about it, Kelly. He may want to handle this himself.

KELLY. He'll be furious. I know he will. He'll die. And then he'll terminate me.

SANDERSON. (*Below table, catches her shoulders.*) The responsibility is all mine, Kelly.

KELLY. Oh, no—tell him it was all my fault, Doctor.

SANDERSON. I never mention your name. (*Crossing to door* R.) Except in my sleep.

17

KELLY. But this man Dowd —— (*Kneels on chair* R.)

SANDERSON. Don't let him get away. I'll be right back.

KELLY. (*Crosses to* L. *of chair* R. *of table*.) But what shall I say to him? What shall I do? He'll be furious.

SANDERSON. Look, Kelly—he'll probably be fit to be tied—but he's a man, isn't he?

KELLY. I guess so—his name is Mister. (*Off chair.*)

SANDERSON. (*Across chair from her.*) Go into your old routine —you know—the eyes—the swish—the works. I'm immune— but I've seen it work with some people—some of the patients out here. Keep him here, Kelly—if you have to do a strip tease. (*He exits* R.)

KELLY. (*Very angry. Speaks to closed door.*) Well, of all the— oh—you're wonderful, Dr. Sanderson! You're just about the most wonderful person I ever met in my life. (*Kicks chair.*)

WILSON. (*Has entered from* C. *in time to hear last sentence.*) Yeah—but how about giving me a lift here just the same?

KELLY. What?

WILSON. That Simmons dame.

KELLY. (*Crosses to Wilson.*) Did you catch her?

WILSON. Slick as a whistle. She was comin' along the path hummin' a little tune. I jumped out at her from behind a tree. I says "Sister—there's a man wants to see you." Shoulda heard her yell! She's whacky, all right.

KELLY. Take her to No. 13 upper West R: (*Crosses* WILSON *to back of desk.*)

WILSON. She's there now. Brought her in through the diet kitchen. She's screamin' and kickin' like hell. I'll hold her if you'll come and undress her.

KELLY. Just a second, Wilson. Dr. Sanderson told me to stay here till her brother comes down—(*Round back of desk.*)

WILSON. Make it snappy—(*Goes out* C. ELWOOD *enters* C. KELLY *rises.*)

KELLY. You're Mr. Dowd?

ELWOOD. (*Carrying other hat and coat over his arm. He bows.*) Elwood P.

KELLY. I'm Miss Kelly.

ELWOOD. Let me give you one of my cards. (*Fishes in vest pocket—pulls out card.*) If you should want to call me—call me at this number. Don't call me at that one. That's the old one.

KELLY. Thank you.

18

ELWOOD. Perfectly all right, and if you lose it—don't worry, my dear. I have plenty more.

KELLY. Won't you have a chair, please, Mr. Dowd?

ELWOOD. Thank you. I'll have two. Allow me. (*He brings another chair down from* U.C. *to* L. *of chair* L. *of table. Puts extra hat and coat on table* C. *Motions Harvey to sit in chair* L. *of table. He stands waiting.*)

KELLY. Dr. Sanderson is very anxious to talk to you. He'll be here in a minute. Please be seated.

ELWOOD. (*Waving her toward chair* R. *of desk.*) After you, my dear.

KELLY. Oh, I really can't, thank you. I'm in and out all the time. But you mustn't mind me. Please sit down.

ELWOOD. (*Bowing.*) After you.

KELLY. (*She sits chair* R. *of desk. He sits on chair he has just put in place.*) Could I get you a magazine to look at?

ELWOOD. I would much rather look at you, Miss Kelly, if you don't mind. You really are very lovely.

KELLY. Oh—well. Thank you. Some people don't seem to think so.

ELWOOD. Some people are blind. That is often brought to my attention. And now, Miss Kelly—I would like to have you meet—(*Enter* SANDERSON *from* R. MISS KELLY *rises and backs up to below desk.* ELWOOD *rises when she does, and he makes a motion to the invisible Harvey to rise, too.*)

SANDERSON. (*Going to him, extending hand.*) Mr. Dowd?

ELWOOD. Elwood P. Let me give you one of my cards. If you should want—

SANDERSON. (*Crossing to* C.) Mr. Dowd—I am Dr. Lyman Sanderson, Dr. Chumley's assistant out here.

ELWOOD. Well, good for you! I'm happy to know you. How are you, Doctor?

SANDERSON. That's going to depend on you, I'm afraid. Please sit down. You've met Miss Kelly, Mr. Dowd?

ELWOOD. I have had that pleasure, and I want both of you to meet a very dear friend of mine—

SANDERSON. Later on—be glad to. Won't you be seated, because first I want to say—

ELWOOD. After Miss Kelly—

SANDERSON. Sit down, Kelly—(SHE *sits* L. *of desk, as does* ELWOOD—*who indicates to Harvey to sit also.*) Is that chair quite comfortable, Mr. Dowd?

19

ELWOOD. Yes, thank you. Would you care to try it? (*He takes out a cigarette.*)

SANDERSON. No, thank you. How about an ash tray there? Could we give Mr. Dowd an ash tray? (KELLY *gets up—gets it from wall L.* ELWOOD *and Harvey rise also.* ELWOOD *beams as he turns and watches her.* KELLY *puts ash tray by* DOWD, *who moves it to share with Harvey.*) Is it too warm in here for you, Mr. Dowd? Would you like me to open a window? (ELWOOD *hasn't heard. He is watching Miss Kelly.*)

KELLY. (*Turning, smiling at him.*) Mr. Dowd—Dr. Sanderson wants to know if he should open a window?

ELWOOD. That's entirely up to him. I wouldn't presume to live his life for him. (*During this dialogue* SANDERSON *is near window.* KELLY *has her eyes on his face.* ELWOOD *smiles at Harvey fondly.* KELLY *sits at L. of desk.*)

SANDERSON. Now then, Mr. Dowd, I can see that you're not the type of person to be taken in by any high-flown phrases or beating about the bush. (*Sits on lower R. corner of desk.*)

ELWOOD. (*Politely.*) Is that so, Doctor?

SANDERSON. You have us at a disadvantage here. You know it. We know it. Let's lay the cards on the table.

ELWOOD. That certainly appeals to me, Doctor.

SANDERSON. Best way in the long run. People are people, no matter where you go.

ELWOOD. That is very often the case.

SANDERSON. And being human are therefore liable to mistakes. Miss Kelly and I have made a mistake here this afternoon, Mr. Dowd, and we'd like to explain it to you.

KELLY. It wasn't Doctor Sanderson's fault, Mr. Dowd. It was mine.

SANDERSON. A human failing—as I said.

ELWOOD. I find it very interesting, nevertheless. You and Miss Kelly here? (THEY *nod.*) This afternoon—you say? (THEY *nod.* ELWOOD *gives Harvey a knowing look.*)

KELLY. We do hope you'll understand, Mr. Dowd.

ELWOOD. Oh, yes. Yes. These things are often the basis of a long and warm friendship.

SANDERSON. And the responsibility is, of course, not hers—but mine.

ELWOOD. Your attitude may be old-fashioned, Doctor—but I like it.

SANDERSON. Now, if I had seen your sister first—that would

have been an entirely different story.

ELWOOD. Now there you surprise me. I think the world and all of Veta—but I had supposed she had seen her day. (KELLY *sits chair* R. *of desk.*)

SANDERSON. You must not attach any blame to her. She is a very sick woman. Came in here insisting you were in need of treatment. That's perfectly ridiculous.

ELWOOD. Veta shouldn't be upset about me. I get along fine.

SANDERSON. Exactly—but your sister had already talked to Miss Kelly, and there had been a call from your family lawyer, Judge Gaffney—

ELWOOD. Oh, yes, I know him. Know his wife, too. Nice people. (*He turns to Harvey—cigarette business: he needs a match.*)

SANDERSON. Is there something I can get for you, Mr. Dowd?

ELWOOD. What did you have in mind?

SANDERSON. A light—here—let me give you a light. (*Crosses to* DOWD, *lights his cigarette.* ELWOOD *brushes smoke away from the rabbit.*) Your sister was extremely nervous and plunged right away into a heated tirade on your drinking. (*Crosses back to sit on chair* R. *of desk.*)

ELWOOD. That was Veta.

SANDERSON. She became hysterical.

ELWOOD. I tell Veta not to worry about that. I'll take care of that.

SANDERSON. Exactly. Oh, I suppose you take a drink now and then—the same as the rest of us?

ELWOOD. Yes, I do. As a matter of fact, I would like one right now.

SANDERSON. Matter of fact, so would I, but your sister's reaction to the whole matter of drinking was entirely too intense. Does your sister drink, Mr. Dowd?

ELWOOD. Oh, no, Doctor. No. I don't believe Veta has ever taken a drink.

SANDERSON. Well, I'm going to surprise you. I think she has and does—constantly.

ELWOOD. I am certainly surprised.

SANDERSON. But it's not her alcoholism that's going to be the basis for my diagnosis of her case. It's much more serious than that. It was when she began talking so emotionally about this big white rabbit—Harvey—yes, I believe she called him Harvey—

21

ELWOOD. (*Nodding.*) Harvey is his name.

SANDERSON. She claimed you were persecuting her with this Harvey.

ELWOOD. I haven't been persecuting her with Harvey. Veta shouldn't feel that way. And now, Doctor, before we go any further I must insist you let me introduce—(*He starts to rise.*)

SANDERSON. Let me make my point first, Mr. Dowd. This trouble of your sister's didn't spring up overnight. Her condition stems from trauma.

ELWOOD. (*Sits down again.*) From what?

SANDERSON. From trauma.—Spelled T-R-A-U-M-A. It means shock. Nothing unusual about it. There is the birth trauma. The shock to the act of being born.

ELWOOD. (*Nodding.*) That's the one we never get over—

SANDERSON. You have a nice sense of humor, Dowd—hasn't he, Miss Kelly?

KELLY. Oh, yes, Doctor.

ELWOOD. May I say the same about both of you?

SANDERSON. To sum it all up—your sister's condition is serious, but I can help her. She must however remain out here temporarily.

ELWOOD. I've always wanted Veta to have everything she needs.

SANDERSON. Exactly.

ELWOOD. But I wouldn't want Veta to stay out here unless she liked it out here and wanted to stay here.

SANDERSON. Of course. (*To Kelly.*) Did Wilson get what he went after? (KELLY *nods.*)

KELLY. Yes, Doctor. (*She rises.*)

SANDERSON. What was Mrs. Simmons' attitude, Miss Kelly?

KELLY. (*Crosses above desk to file cabinet* R.) Not unusual, Doctor.

SANDERSON. (*Rising.*) Mr. Dowd, if this were an ordinary delusion—something reflected on the memory picture—in other words, if she were seeing something she had seen once—that would be one thing. But this is more serious. It stands to reason nobody has ever seen a white rabbit six feet high.

ELWOOD. (*Smiles at Harvey.*) Not very often, Doctor.

SANDERSON. I like you, Dowd.

ELWOOD. I like you, too, Doctor. And Miss Kelly here. (*Looks*

for MISS KELLEY, *who is just crossing in front of window seat.*
ELWOOD *springs to his feet.* KELLY *sits quickly.* ELWOOD *motions Harvey down and sits, himself.*) I like her, too.

SANDERSON. So she must be committed here temporarily. Under these circumstances I would commit my own grandmother. (*Goes to* L. *of desk.*)

ELWOOD. Does your grandmother drink, too?

SANDERSON. It's just an expression. (*Leans over desk.*) Now will you sign these temporary commitment papers as next-of-kin—just a formality?

ELWOOD. (*Rises, crosses to* R. *of desk.*) You'd better have Veta do that, Doctor. She always does all the signing and managing for the family. She's good at it. (*Pushes chair* R. *of desk under desk.*)

SANDERSON. We can't disturb her now. (*Sits* L. *of desk.*)

ELWOOD. Perhaps I'd better talk it over with Judge Gaffney?

SANDERSON. You can explain it all to him later. Tell him I advised it. And it isn't as if you couldn't drop in here any time and make inquiries. Glad to have you. I'll make out a full visitor's pass for you. When would you like to come back? Wednesday, say? Friday, say?

ELWOOD. You and Miss Kelly have been so pleasant I can come back right after dinner. About an hour.

SANDERSON. (*Taken aback.*) Well—we're pretty busy around here, but I guess that's all right.

ELWOOD. I don't really have to go now. I'm not very hungry.

SANDERSON. Delighted to have you stay—but Miss Kelly and I have to get on upstairs now. Plenty of work to do. But I tell you what you might like to do.

ELWOOD. What might I like to do?

SANDERSON. We don't usually do this—but just to make sure in your mind that your sister is in good hands—why don't you look around here? If you go through that door—(*Rises—points beyond stairway.*) and turn right just beyond the stairway you'll find the occupational therapy room down the hall, and beyond that the conservatory, the library and the diet kitchen.

ELWOOD. For Veta's sake I believe I'd better do that, Doctor.

SANDERSON. Very well, then. (*He is now anxious to terminate the interview. Rises, shakes hands.*) It's been a great pleasure to have this little talk with you, Mr. Dowd. (*Gives him pass.*)

ELWOOD. (*Walking toward her.*) I've enjoyed it too, Doctor—meeting you and Miss Kelly.

SANDERSON. And I will say that for a layman you show an unusually acute perception into psychiatric problems.

ELWOOD. Is that a fact? I never thought I knew anything about it. Nobody does, do you think?

SANDERSON. Well—the good psychiatrist is not found under every bush.

ELWOOD. You have to pick the right bush. Since we all seem to have enjoyed this so much, let us keep right on. I would like to invite you to come with me now down to Charlie's Place and have a drink. When I enjoy people I like to stay right with them.

SANDERSON. Sorry—we're on duty now. Give us a rain-check. Some other time be glad to.

ELWOOD. When?

SANDERSON. Oh—can't say right now. Miss Kelly and I don't go off duty till ten o'clock at night.

ELWOOD. Let us go to Charlie's at ten o'clock tonight.

SANDERSON. Well—

ELWOOD. And you, Miss Kelly?

KELLY. I—(*Looks at Sanderson.*)

SANDERSON. Dr. Chumley doesn't approve of members of the staff fraternizing, but since you've been so understanding perhaps we could manage it.

ELWOOD. I'll pick you up out here in a cab at ten o'clock tonight and the four of us will spend a happy evening. I want you both to become friends with a very dear friend of mine. You said later on—so later on it will be. Goodbye, now. (*Motions goodbye to Harvey. Tips hat, exits* C.)

KELLY. (*Places chair and ash tray against back wall.*) Whew—now I can breathe again!

SANDERSON. Boy, that was a close shave all right, but he seemed to be a pretty reasonable sort of fellow. That man is proud—what he has to be proud of I don't know. I played up to that pride. You can get to almost anybody if you want to. Now I must look in on that Simmons woman. (*Crosses below desk toward* C.)

KELLY. (*At* R. C.) Dr. Sanderson—! (SANDERSON *turns.*) You say you can get to anybody if you want to. How can you do that?

SANDERSON. Takes study, Kelly. Years of specialized training.

There's only one thing I don't like about this Dowd business.

KELLY. What's that?

SANDERSON. Having to make that date with him. Of course the man has left here as a good friend and booster of this sanitarium—so I guess I'll have to go with him tonight—but you don't have to go.

KELLY. Oh! (*Back of chair* L. *of table.*)

SANDERSON. No point in it. I'll have a drink with him, pat him on the back and leave. I've got a date tonight, anyway.

KELLY. (*Freezing.*) Oh, yes—by all means. I didn't intend to go, anyway. The idea bored me stiff. I wouldn't go if I never went anywhere again. I wouldn't go if my life depended on it.

SANDERSON. (*Stepping back to her.*) What's the matter with you, Kelly? What are you getting so emotional about?

KELLY. He may be a peculiar man with funny clothes, but he knows how to act. His manners were perfect.

SANDERSON. I saw you giving him the doll-puss stare. I didn't miss that.

KELLY. He wouldn't sit down till I sat down. He told me I was lovely and he called me dear. I'd go to have a drink with him if you weren't going.

SANDERSON. Sure you would. And look at him! All he does is hang around bars. He doesn't work. All that corny bowing and getting up out of his chair every time a woman makes a move. Why, he's as outdated as a cast-iron deer. But you'd sit with him in a bar and let him flatter you.—You're a wonderful girl, Kelly.

KELLY. Now let me tell you something—you— (*Enter from down* R. *the great* DR. WILLIAM CHUMLEY. DR. CHUMLEY *is a large, handsome man of about 57. He has gray hair and wears rimless glasses which he removes now and then to tap on his hand for emphasis. He is smartly dressed. His manner is confident, pompous and lordly. He is good and he knows it*).

CHUMLEY. (*Enters with book.*) Dr. Sanderson! Miss Kelly! (THEY *break apart and jump to attention like two buck privates before a* C.O.)

KELLY AND SANDERSON. Yes, Doctor?

CHUMLEY. Tell the gardener to prune more carefully around my prize dahlias along the fence by the main road. They'll be ready for cutting next week. (*At upper corner of bookcase.*) The difficulty of the woman who has the big white rabbit—has it been smoothed over?

SANDERSON. Yes, Doctor. I spoke to her brother and he was quite reasonable.

CHUMLEY. While I have had many patients out here who saw animals, I have never before had a patient with an animal that large. (*Puts book in book-case.*)

SANDERSON. Yet, Doctor. She called him Harvey.

CHUMLEY. Harvey. Unusual name for an animal of any kind. Harvey is a man's name. I have known several men in my day named Harvey, but I have never heard of any type of animal whatsoever with that name. The case has an interesting phase, Doctor. (*Finishes straightening books.*)

SANDERSON. Yes, Doctor.

CHUMLEY. I will now go upstairs with you and look in on this woman. It may be that we can use my formula 977 on her. I will give you my advice in prescribing the treatment, Doctor. (*Crosses to below table.*)

SANDERSON. Thank you, Doctor.

CHUMLEY. (*Starts to move across stage toward* C. *and stops, draws himself up sternly.*) And now—may I ask—what is that hat and coat doing on that table? Whose is it?

SANDERSON. I don't know. Do you know, Miss Kelly? Was it Dowd's?

KELLY. (*Above table, picking up hat and coat.*) He had his hat on, Doctor. Perhaps it belongs to a relative of one of the patients.

CHUMLEY. (*Crosses to* C.) *Hand me the hat.* (KELLY *hands it. Looking inside:*) There may be some kind of identification— Here—what's this—what's this? (*Pushes two fingers up through the holes.*) Two holes cut in the crown of this hat. See!

KELLY. That's strange!

CHUMLEY. Some new fad—put them away. Hang them up— get them out of here. (KELLY *takes them into upper* L. *office.* CHUMLEY *starts crossing to table.* KELLY *has come out of* L. WILSON *comes in through* C.)

WILSON. (*Very impressed with Dr. Chumley and very fond of him.*) Hello, Dr. Chumley.

CHUMLEY. Oh, there you are.

WILSON. How is every little old thing? (DR. CHUMLEY *picks up pad of notes from* R. *of desk;* R. *of table, looking at notes.* KELLY *re-enters from upper left.*)

CHUMLEY. Fair, thank you, Wilson, fair.

WILSON. (*Top of desk.*) Look—somebody's gonna have to give me a hand with this Simmons dame—order a restraining jacket or something. She's terrible. (*To Kelly.*) *Forgot me,* didn't you? Well, I got her corset off all by myself.

CHUMLEY. We're going up to see this patient right now, Wilson.

WILSON. She's in a hydro tub now—my God—I left the water *running on her!* (*Runs off* C. *upstairs, followed by* KELLY.) (BETTY CHUMLEY, *the Doctor's wife, enters down* L. *She is a good-natured, gay, bustling woman of about 55.*)

BETTY. Willie—remember your promise—. Hello, Dr. Sanderson. Willie, you haven't forgotten Dr. McClure's cocktail *party? We promised them faithfully.* (*Sits* L. *of table* R.)

CHUMLEY. That's right. I have to go upstairs now and look in on a patient. Be down shortly— (*Exits* C. *upstairs.*)

BETTY. (*Calling after him; as she crosses down to chair* L. *of table, she sits, fixes her shoe.*) Give a little quick diagnosis, Willie—we don't want to be late to the party. I'm dying to see the inside of that house. (*Enter* ELWOOD *from* C. *He doesn't see Betty at first. He looks around the room carefully.*) Good evening.

ELWOOD. (*Removing his hat and bowing.*) Good evening. (*Puts hat on desk. Walks over to her.*)

BETTY. I am Mrs. Chumley. Doctor Chumley's wife.

ELWOOD. I'm happy to know that. Dowd is my name. Elwood P. Let me give you one of my cards. (*Gives her one.*) If you should want to call me—call me at this one. Don't call me at that one, because that's—(*Points at card*) the old one. (*Starts one step. Looking.*)

BETTY. Thank you. Is there something I can do for you?

ELWOOD. (*Turns to her.*) What did you have in mind?

BETTY. You seem to be looking for someone.

ELWOOD. (*Walking.*) Yes, I am. I'm looking for Harvey. I went off without him.

BETTY. Harvey? Is he a patient here?

ELWOOD. (*Turns.*) Oh, no. Nothing like that. (*Cross to door down* L.)

BETTY. Does he work here?

ELWOOD. (*Looking out down* L. *door.*) Oh no. He is what you might call my best friend. He is also a pooka. He came out

27

here with me and Veta this afternoon.

BETTY. Where was he when you last saw him?

ELWOOD. (*Behind chair L. of desk.*) In that chair there—with his hat and coat on the table.

BETTY. There doesn't seem to be any hat and coat around here now. Perhaps he left?

ELWOOD. Apparently. I don't see him anywhere. (*Looks in* SANDERSON'S *office.*)

BETTY. What was that word you just said—pooka?

ELWOOD. (*Crosses C. He is looking in hallway C.*) Yes—that's it.

BETTY. Is that something new? (*Looks in hallway.*)

ELWOOD. (*Coming down.*) Oh, no. As I understand it. That's something very old.

BETTY. Oh, really? I had never happened to hear it before.

ELWOOD. I'm not too surprised at that. I hadn't myself, until I met him. I do hope you get an opportunity to meet him. I'm sure he would be quite taken with you. (*Down C. on a line with Betty.*)

BETTY. Oh, really? Well, that's very nice of you to say so, I'm sure.

ELWOOD. Not at all. If Harvey happens to take a liking to people he expresses himself quite definitely. If he's not particularly interested, he sits there like an empty chair or an empty space on the floor. Harvey takes his time making his mind up about people. Choosey, you see. (*Crosses above table to door R.*)

BETTY. That's not such a bad way to be in this day and age.

ELWOOD. Harvey is fond of my sister, Veta. That's because he is fond of me, and Veta and I come from the same family. Now you'd think that feeling would be mutual, wouldn't you? (*Looks in office R. Crosses to chair R. of table.*) But Veta doesn't seem to care for Harvey. Don't you think that's rather too bad, Mrs. Chumley?

BETTY. Oh, I don't know, Mr. Dowd. I gave up a long time ago expecting my family to like my friends. It's useless.

ELWOOD. But we must keep on trying. (*Sits chair R. of table.*)

BETTY. Well, there's no harm in trying, I suppose.

ELWOOD. Because if Harvey has said to me once he has said a million times—"Mr. Dowd, I would do anything for you." Mrs. Chumley—

BETTY. Yes—

ELWOOD. Did you know that Mrs. McElinney's Aunt Rose is going to drop in on her unexpectedly tonight from Cleveland?

BETTY. Why, no I didn't —

ELWOOD. Neither does she. That puts you both in the same boat, doesn't it?

BETTY. Well, I don't know anybody named—Mrs.——

ELWOOD. Mrs. McElhinney? Lives next door to us. She is a wonderful woman. Harvey told me about her Aunt Rose. That's an interesting little news item, and you are perfectly free to pass it around.

BETTY. Well, I ——

ELWOOD. Would you care to come downtown with me now, my dear? I would be glad to buy you a drink.

BETTY. Thank you very much, but I am waiting for Dr. Chumley and if he came down and found me gone he would be liable to raise—he would be irritated!

ELWOOD. We wouldn't want that, would me? Some other time, maybe? (*He rises.*)

BETTY. I'll tell you what I'll do, however.

ELWOOD. What will you do, however? I'm interested.

BETTY. If your friend comes in while I'm here I'd be glad to give him a message for you.

ELWOOD. (*Gratefully.*) Would you do that? I'd certainly appreciate that. (*Goes up C. to top of desk for his hat.*)

BETTY. No trouble at all. I'll write it down on the back of this. (*Holds up card. Takes pencil from purse.*) What would you like me to tell him if he comes in while I'm still here?

ELWOOD. Ask him to meet me downtown—if he has no other plans.

BETTY. (*Writing.*) Meet Mr. Dowd downtown. Any particular place down-town?

ELWOOD. He knows where. Harvey knows this town like a book.

BETTY. (*Writing.*) Harvey—you know where. Harvey what?

ELWOOD. Just Harvey.

BETTY. (*Rises—crosses to desk.*) I'll tell you what.

ELWOOD. What?

BETTY. (*Swings chair R. of desk in position.*) Doctor and I are going right down-town—to 12th and Moneview. Dr. McClure is having a cocktail party.

ELWOOD. (*At* L. *of desk; he writes that down on pad on desk.*) A cocktail party at 12th and Montview.

BETTY. We're driving there in a few minutes. We could give your friend a lift into town.

ELWOOD. I hate to impose on you—but I would certainly appreciate that.

BETTY. No trouble at all. Dr. McClure is having this party for his sister from Wichita.

ELWOOD. I didn't know Dr. McClure had a sister in Wichita.

BETTY. Oh—you *know* Dr. McClure?

ELWOOD. No.

BETTY. (*Puts Elwood's card down on desk.*) But —— (*Sits chair* R. *of desk.*)

ELWOOD. You're quite sure you haven't time to come into town with me and have a drink?

BETTY. I really couldn't—but thank you just the same.

ELWOOD. Some other time, perhaps?

BETTY. Thank you.

ELWOOD. It's been very pleasant to meet you, and I hope to see you again.

BETTY. Yes, so do I.

ELWOOD. Goodnight, my dear. (*Tips hat—bows—goes to door, turns.*) You can't miss Harvey. He's very tall—(*Shows with hands.*) Like that—(*Exits down* L. *From back* C. *now comes* CHUMLEY, *followed by* SANDERSON *and* KELLY. CHUMLEY *goes to chair* R. *of desk.* KELLY *crosses above table to* R. C. *office for Chumley's hat and coat.* SANDERSON *goes to top of desk.*)

CHUMLEY. (*Working with pen on desk-pad.*) That Simmons woman is uncooperative, Doctor. She refused to admit to me that she has this big rabbit. Insists it's her brother. Give her two of these at nine—another at ten—if she continues to be so restless. Another trip to the hydro-room at eight, and one in the morning at seven. Then we'll see if she won't cooperate tomorrow, won't we, Doctor?

SANDERSON. Yes, Doctor.

CHUMLEY. (*Putting pen away.*) You know where to call me if you need me. Ready, pet?

BETTY. Yes, Willie—and oh, Willie—

CHUMLEY. Yes—

BETTY. There was a man in here—a man named—let me see— (*Picks up card from desk.*) Oh, here is his card—Dowd—Elwood P. Dowd. KELLY *enters from* R. *to below table—she has Dr. Chumley's hat.*)

SANDERSON. That's Mrs. Simmons' brother, Doctor. I told him he could look around, and I gave him full visiting privileges.

CHUMLEY. She mustn't see anyone tonight. Not anyone at all. Tell him that.

SANDERSON. Yes, Doctor.

BETTY. He didn't ask to see her? He was looking for someone —some friend of his.

CHUMLEY. Who could that be, Dr. Sanderson?

SANDERSON. I don't know, Doctor.

BETTY. He said it was someone he came out here with this afternoon.

SANDERSON. Was there anyone with Dowd when you saw him, Miss Kelly?

KELLY. (R. C. *giving hat to* SANDERSON.) No, Doctor—not when I saw him.

BETTY. Well, he said there was. He said he last saw his friend sitting right in that chair there with his hat and coat. He seemed quite disappointed.

KELLY. (*At top of table—a funny look is crossing her face.*) Dr. Sanderson—

BETTY. I told him if we located his friend we'd give him a lift into town. He could ride in the back seat. Was that all right, Willie?

CHUMLEY. Of course—of course—

BETTY. Oh here it is. I wrote it down on the back of this card. His friend's name was Harvey.

KELLY. Harvey!

BETTY. He didn't give me his last name. He mentioned something else about him—pooka—but I didn't quite get what that was.

SANDERSON *and* CHUMLEY. Harvey!

BETTY. (*Rises.*) He said his friend was very tall—. Well, why are you looking like that, Willie? This man was a very nice, polite man, and he merely asked that we give his friend a lift into town, and if we can't do a favor for someone, why are we living? (*Back to down* R.)

SANDERSON. (*Gasping.*) Where—where did he go, Mrs. Chumley? How long ago was he in here?

CHUMLEY. (*Thundering.*) Get me that hat! By George, we'll find out about this! (KELLY *goes out upper* L. *to get it.* BETTY *crosses* R. *to chair* R. *of table.* CHUMLEY *and* SANDERSON *sit at* R. *of desk.*)

BETTY. I don't know where he went. Just a second ago. (SANDERSON, *his face drawn, sits at* L. *of desk and picks up house phone.* CHUMLEY, *with a terrible look on his face, has started to thumb through phone book.*)

SANDERSON. (*On house phone.*) Main gate—Henry—Dr. Sanderson—

CHUMLEY. (*Thumbing through book.*) Gaffney—Judge Gaffney ——

SANDERSON. Henry—did a man in a brown suit go out through the gate a minute ago? He did? He's gone? (*Hangs up and looks stricken.* KELLY *enters from* L. *with hat, comes* C.)

CHUMLEY. (*Has been dialing.*) Judge Gaffney—this is Dr. William Chumley—the psychiatrist. I'm making a routine check-up on the spelling of a name before entering it into our records. Judge—you telephoned out here this afternoon about having a client of yours committed? How is that name spelled? With a W, not a U—Mr. Elwood P. Dowd. Thank you, Judge—(*Hangs up—rises—pushes chair in to desk—takes hat from* KELLY. *Stands silently for a moment, contemplating* SANDERSON.) Dr. Sanderson—I believe your name is Sanderson?

SANDERSON. Yes, Doctor.

CHUMLEY. You know that much, do you? You went to medical school—you specialized in the study of psychiatry? You graduated—you went forth. (*Holds up hat and runs two fingers up through holes in it.*) Perhaps they neglected to tell you that a rabbit has large pointed ears! That a hat for a rabbit would have to be perforated to make room for those ears?

SANDERSON. Dowd seemed reasonable enough this afternoon, Doctor.

CHUMLEY. Doctor—the function of a psychiatrist is to tell the difference between those who are reasonable, and those who merely talk and act reasonably. (*Presses buzzer. Flings hat on desk.*) Do you realize what you have done to me? You don't answer. I'll tell you. You have permitted a psycopathic case to walk off these grounds and roam around with an overgrown white rabbit. You have subjected me—a psychiatrist—to the humiliation of having to call—of all things—a lawyer to find out who came out here to be committed—and who came out here to commit! (WILSON *enters.*)

SANDERSON. Dr. Chumley—I—

CHUMLEY. Just a minute, Wilson—I want you. (*Back to* SAN-DERSON.) I will now have to do something I haven't done in fifteen years. I will have to go out after this patient, Elwood P. Dowd, and I will have to bring him back, and when I do bring him, back your connection with this institution is ended—as of that moment! (*Turns to* WILSON—OTHERS *are standing frightened.*) Wilson, get the car. (*To* BETTY.) Pet, call the McClures and say we can't make it. Miss Kelly—come upstairs with me and we'll get that woman out of the tub— (*Starts upstairs on the run.*)

KELLY. (*Follows him upstairs.*) Yes—Doctor——(SANDERSON *turns on his heel, goes into his office.* WILSON *is getting into a coat in hall.*)

BETTY. (*At bookcase* R.) I'll have to tell the cook we'll be home for dinner. She'll be furious. (*She turns.*) Wilson ——

WILSON. Yes, ma'am.

BETTY. What is a pooka?

WILSON. A what?

BETTY. A pooka.

WILSON. You can search me, Mrs. Chumley.

BETTY. I wonder if it would be in the Encyclopedia here? (*Goes to bookcase and takes out book.*) They have everything here. I wonder if it is a lodge, or what it is! (*Starts to look in it, then puts it on table open.*) Oh, I don't dare to stop to do this now. Dr. Chumley won't want to find me still here when he comes down. (*Starts to cross to lower* L. *door very fast.*) He'll raise—I mean—oh, dear! (*She exits down* L.)

WILSON. (*Goes above tables picks up book, looks in it. Runs forefinger under words.*) P-o-o-k-a. "Pooka. From old Celtic mythology. A fairy spirit in animal form. Always very large. The pooka appears here and there, now and then, to this one and that one at his own caprice. A wise but mischievous creature. Very fond of rum-pots, crack-pots," and how are you, Mr. Wilson. (*Looks at book startled—looks at* C. *doorway fearfully—then back to book.*) How are you, Mr. Wilson? (*Shakes book, looks at it in surprise.*) Who in the encyclopedia wants to know? (*Looks at book again, drops it on table.*) Oh—to hell with it! (*He exits quickly out down* L.)

CURTAIN

ACT II

SCENE 1

SCENE: *The Dowd library again.*
TIME: *About an hour after the curtain of Act I.*
AT RISE: *Doorbell is ringing and* MYRTLE *enters from door up* L. *She calls behind her.*

MYRTLE. (*Calling.*) That's right. The stairs at the end of the hall. It goes to the third floor. Go right up. I'll be with you in a minute. (*Crosses to chair* L. *of table.* JUDGE OMAR GAFFNEY *enters* R., *an elderly white-haired man. He looks displeased.*)
JUDGE. (*Entering and looking around.*) Well, where is she? (*Back of table.*)
MYRTLE. Where is who? Whom do you mean, Judge Gaffney? Sit down, won't you?
JUDGE. I mean your mother. Where's Veta Louise? (*Crosses in front of chair.*)
MYRTLE. Why Judge Gaffney! You know where she is. She took Uncle Elwood out to the sanitarium.
JUDGE. I know that. But why was I called at the club with a lot of hysteria? Couldn't even get what she was talking about. Carrying on something fierce. (*Sits chair* R. *of table* R.)
MYRTLE. Mother carrying on! What about? (*Crosses down to chair* L. *of table* R.)
JUDGE. I don't know. She was hysterical.
MYRTLE. That's strange! She took Uncle Elwood out to the sanitarium. All she had to do was put him in. (*Goes back* R., *opens door and looks through, calling.*) Did you find it? I'll be right up. (*Waits. Turns to him.*) They found it.
JUDGE. Who? Found what? What are you talking about?
MYRTLE. When Mother left the house with Uncle Elwood I went over to the real estate office to put the house on the market. And what do you think I found there? (*She sits.*)
JUDGE. I'm not a quiz kid.
MYRTLE. Well, I found a man there who was looking for an old house just like this to cut up into buffet apartments. He's

34

going through it now.

JUDGE. Now see here, Myrtle Mae. This house doesn't belong to you. It belongs to your Uncle Elwood.

MYRTLE. But now that Elwood is locked up. Mother controls the property, doesn't she?

JUDGE. Where is your mother? Where is Veta Louise?

MYRTLE. Judge, she went out to Chumley's Rest to tell them about Harvey and put Uncle Elwood in.

JUDGE. Why did she call me at the club when I was in the middle of a game, and scream at me to meet her here about something important?

MYRTLE. I don't know. I simply don't know. Have you got the deed to this house?

JUDGE. Certainly, it's in my safe. Myrtle, I feel pretty bad about this thing of locking Elwood up.

MYRTLE. Mother and I will be able to take a long trip now— out to Pasadena.

JUDGE. I always liked that boy. He could have done anything —been anything—made a place for himself in this community.

MYRTLE. And all he did was get a big rabbit.

JUDGE. He had everything. Brains, personality, friends. Men liked him. Women liked him. I liked him.

MYRTLE. Are you telling me that once Uncle Elwood was like other men—that women actually liked him—I mean in that way?

JUDGE. Oh, not since he started running around with this big rabbit. But they did once. Once that mail-box of your grandmother's was full of those little blue-scented envelopes for Elwood.

MYRTLE. I can't believe it.

JUDGE. Of course there was always something different about Elwood.

MYRTLE. I don't doubt that.

JUDGE. Yes—he was always so calm about any sudden change in plans. I used to admire it. I should have been suspicious. Take your average man looking up and seeing a big white rabbit. He'd do something about it. But not Elwood. He took that calmly, too. And look where it got him!

MYRTLE. You don't dream how far overboard he's gone on

this rabbit.

JUDGE. Oh, yes I do. He's had that rabbit in my office many's the time. I'm old but I don't miss much. (*Noise from upstairs.*) What's that noise?

MYRTLE. The prospective buyer on the third floor. (*Looks up. VETA is standing in doorway, looking like something the cat dragged in. Shakes her head sadly; looks into the room and sighs; her hat is crooked. MYRTLE jumps up.*) Mother! Look, Judge—

JUDGE. (*Rising.*) Veta Louise—what's wrong, girl?

VETA. (*Shaking her head.*) I never thought I'd see either of you again. (*MYRTLE and JUDGE take VETA to chair L. of table R.*)

MYRTLE. Take hold of her, Judge. She looks like she's going to faint. (*JUDGE gets hold of her on one side and MYRTLE on the other. They start to bring her into the room.*) Now, Mother—you're all right. You're going to be perfectly all right.

JUDGE. Steady—steady, girl, steady.

VETA. Please—not so fast.

JUDGE. Don't rush her, Myrtle—Ease her in.

VETA. Let me sit down. Only get me some place where I can sit down.

JUDGE. (*Guiding her to a big chair.*) Here you are, girl. Easy, Myrtle—easy. (*VETA is about to lower herself into chair. She sighs. But before she can complete the lowering, MYRTLE MAE lets out a yelp and VETA straightens up quickly.*)

MYRTLE. Oh—(*She picks up envelope off chair. Holds it up.*) The gas bill.

VETA. (*Hand at head.*) Oh—oh, my— (*Sits.*)

JUDGE. Get her some tea, Myrtle. Do you want some tea, Veta?

MYRTLE. I'll get you some tea, Mother. Get her coat off, Judge.

JUDGE. Let Myrtle get your coat off, Veta. Get her coat off, Myrtle.

VETA. Leave me alone. Let me sit here. Let me get my breath.

MYRTLE. Let her get her breath, Judge.

VETA. Let me sit here a minute and then let me get upstairs to my own bed where I can let go.

MYRTLE. What happened to you, Mother?

VETA. Omar, I want you to sue them. They put me in and let

Elwood out.

JUDGE. What's this?

MYRTLE. Mother!

VETA. (*Taking off hat.*) Just look at my hair.

MYRTLE. But why? What did you say? What did you do? (*Kneels at* VETA's *feet.*) You must have done something.

VETA. I didn't do one thing. I simply told them about Elwood and Harvey.

JUDGE. Then how could it happen to you? I don't understand it. (*Sits chair* R.)

VETA. I told them about Elwood, and then I went down to the cab to get his things. As I was walking along the path—this awful man stepped out. He was a white slaver. I know he was. He had on one of those white suits. That's how they advertise.

MYRTLE. A man—what did he do, Mother?

VETA. What did he do? He took hold of me and took me in there and then he —— (*Bows her head.* MYRTLE *and* JUDGE *exchange a look.*)

JUDGE. (*Softly.*) Go on, Veta Louise. Go on, girl.

MYRTLE. (*Goes over, takes her hand.*) Poor Mother —— Was he a young man?

JUDGE. Myrtle Mae—perhaps you'd better leave the room.

MYRTLE. Now? I should say not! Go on, Mother.

JUDGE. (*Edging closer.*) What did he do, Veta?

VETA. He took me upstairs and tore my clothes off.

MYRTLE. (*Shrieking.*) Oh—did you hear that, Judge! Go on, Mother. (*She is all ears.*)

JUDGE. By God—I'll sue them for this!

VETA. And then he sat me down in a tub of water.

MYRTLE. (*Disappointed.*) Oh! For heaven's sake! (*Rises.*)

VETA. I always thought that what you were showed on your face. Don't you believe it, Judge! Don't you believe it, Myrtle. This man took hold of me like I was a woman of the streets—but I fought. I always said if a man jumped at me—I'd fight. Haven't I always said that, Myrtle?

MYRTLE. She's always said that, Judge. That's what Mother always told me to do.

VETA. And then he hustled me into that sanitarium and set me down in that tub of water and began treating me like I was

37

MYRTLE. A what ——?

VETA. A crazy woman—but he did that just for spite.

JUDGE. Well, I'll be damned!

VETA. And those doctors came upstairs and asked me a lot of questions—all about sex-urges—and all that filthy stuff. That place ought to be cleaned up, Omar. You better get the authorities to clean it up. Myrtle, don't you ever go out there. You hear me?

JUDGE. This stinks to high heaven, Veta. By God, it stinks!

VETA. You've got to do something about it, Judge. You've got to sue them.

JUDGE. I will, girl. By God, I will! If Chumley thinks he can run an unsavory place like this on the outskirts of town he'll be publicly chastised. By God, I'll run him out of the State!

VETA. Tell me, Judge. Is that all those doctors do at places like that—think about sex?

JUDGE. I don't know.

VETA. Because if it is they ought to be ashamed—of themselves. It's all in their head anyway. Why don't they get out and go for long walks in the fresh air? (*To* MYRTLE.) Judge Gaffney walked everywhere for years—didn't you, Judge?

JUDGE. Now let me take some notes on this. (MYRTLE *goes to back of table.*) You said—these doctors came up to talk to you—Dr. Chumley and—What was the other doctor's name?

VETA. Sanderson —— (*Sits up straight—glances covertly at them and becomes very alert.*) But, Judge, don't you pay any attention to anything he tells you. He's a liar. Close-set eyes. They're always liars. Besides—I told him something in strictest confidence and he blabbed it.

MYRTLE. What did you tell him, Mother? (*She is back of table.*)

VETA. Oh, what difference does it make? Let's forget it. I don't even want to talk about it. (*Rises—crosses to back of chair.*) You can't trust anybody.

JUDGE. Anything you told this Dr. Sanderson you can tell us, Veta Louise. This is your daughter and I am your lawyer.

VETA. I know which is which. I don't want to talk about it. I want to sue them and I want to get in my own bed. (JUDGE *rises.*)

MYRTLE. But, Mother—this is the important thing, anyway. Where is Uncle Elwood?

VETA. (*To herself.*) I should have known better than to try to do anything about him. Something protects him—that awful Pooka ——

MYRTLE. Where is Uncle Elwood? Answer me.

VETA. (*Trying to be casual.*) How should I know? They let him go. (*Crosses to door* R.) They're not interested in men at places like that. Don't act so naive, Myrtle Mae. (*Noise from upstairs.*) What's that noise?

MYRTLE. I've found a buyer for the house.

VETA. What?

MYRTLE. Listen, Mother, we've got to find Uncle Elwood—no matter who jumped at you we've still got to lock up Uncle Elwood.

VETA. I don't know where he is. The next time *you* take him, Judge. Wait until Elwood hears what they did to me. He won't stand for it. Don't forget to sue them, Judge —— Myrtle Mae, all I hope is that never, never as long as you live a man pulls the clothes off you and dumps you down into a tub of water. (*She exits* R.)

MYRTLE. (*Turning to* JUDGE. *Behind chair* L.) Now, see— Mother muffed everything. No matter what happened out there—Uncle Elwood's still wandering around with Harvey.

JUDGE. (*Pondering.*) The thing for me to do is take some more notes.

MYRTLE. It's all Uncle Elwood's fault. He found out what she was up to—and he had her put in. Then he ran.

JUDGE. Oh, no—don't talk like that. (*Crosses up to back of chair.*) Your uncle thinks the world and all of your mother. Ever since he was a little boy he always wanted to share everything he had with her.

MYRTLE. I'm not giving up. We'll get detectives. We'll find him. And, besides—you'd better save some of that sympathy for me and Mother—you don't realize what we have to put up with. Wait till I show you something he brought home about six months ago, and we hid it out in the garage. You just wait ——

JUDGE. I'm going up to talk to Veta. There's more in this than she's telling. I sense that.

MYRTLE. (*As she exits* L.) Wait till I show you, Judge.

JUDGE. All right. I'll wait. (WILSON *enters from* R.)

WILSON. (*Crosses to table* R.) Okay—is he here?

JUDGE. (*Crosses to chair* R. *of table* R.) What? What's this?

WILSON. That crackpot with the rabbit. Is he here?

JUDGE. No—and who, may I ask, are you?

WILSON. (*Stepping into hallway, calling.*) Not here, Doctor—okay—(*To* JUDGE.) Doctor Chumley's comin' in, anyway. What's your name?

JUDGE. Chumley—well, well, well—I've got something to say to him! (*Sits.*)

WILSON. What's your name? Let's have it.

JUDGE. I am Judge Gaffney—where is Chumley?

WILSON. The reason I asked your name is the Doctor always likes to know who he's talkin' to. (*Enter* CHUMLEY.) This guy says his name is Judge Gaffney, Doctor.

JUDGE. Well, well, Chumley ——

CHUMLEY. Good evening, Judge. Let's not waste time. Has he been here? (*Crosses to* L. *of table.*)

JUDGE. Who? Elwood—no—but see here, Doctor ——

WILSON. Sure he ain't been here? He's wise now. He's hidin'. It'll be an awful job to smoke him out.

CHUMLEY. It will be more difficult, but I'll do it. They're sly. They're cunning. But I get them. I always get them. Have you got the list of the places we've been, Wilson? (*Crosses to* WILSON.)

WILSON. (*Pulling paper out of his pocket.*) Right here, Doctor.

CHUMLEY. (*Sits.*) Read it.

WILSON. (*Crosses to* CHUMLEY.) We've been to seventeen bars, Eddie's Place, Charlie's Place, Bessie's Barn-dance, the Fourth Avenue Firehouse, the Tenth and Twelfth and Ninth Avenue firehouses, just to make sure. The Union Station, the grain elevator—say, why does this guy go down to a grain elevator?

JUDGE. The foreman is a friend of his. He has many friends—many places.

CHUMLEY. I have stopped by here to ask Mrs. Simmons if she has any other suggestions as to where we might look for him.

JUDGE. Doctor Chumley, I have to inform you that Mrs. Simmons has retained me to file suit against you ——

40

DR. CHUMLEY. What?

JUDGE. —for what happened to her at the sanitarium this afternoon . . .

CHUMLEY. A suit!

JUDGE. And while we're on that subject ——

WILSON. (*Crosses to back of table.*) That's pretty, ain't it, Doctor? After us draggin' your tail all over town trying to find that guy.

CHUMLEY. What happened this afternoon was an unfortunate mistake. I've discharged my assistant who made it. And I am prepared to take charge of this man's case personally. It interests me. And my interest in a case is something no amount of money can buy. You can ask any of them.

JUDGE. But this business this afternoon, Doctor ——

CHUMLEY. Water under the dam. This is how I see this thing. I see it this way —— (MYRTLE *has come into the room. She is carrying a big flat parcel, wrapped in brown paper. Stands it up against wall and listens, by chair* L.) The important item now is to get this man and take him out to the sanitarium where he belongs.

MYRTLE. (*Coming forward.*) That's right, Judge—that's just what I think ——

JUDGE. Let me introduce Miss Myrtle Mae Simmons, Mr. Dowd's niece, Mrs. Simmons's daughter. (CHUMLEY *rises.*)

MYRTLE. How do you do, Dr. Chumley.

CHUMLEY. (*Giving her the careful scrutiny he gives all women.*) How do you do, Miss Simmons.

WILSON. Hello, Myrtle ——

MYRTLE. (*Now seeing him and looking at him with a mixture of horror and intense curiosity.*) What? Oh ——

CHUMLEY. Now, then—let me talk to Mrs. Simmons.

MYRTLE. Mother won't come down, Doctor. I know she won't. (*To Judge.*) You try to get Mother to talk to him, Judge. (*Puts package down.*)

JUDGE. But, see here; your mother was manhandled. She was—God knows what she was—the man's approach to her was not professional, it was personal. (*Looks at Wilson.*)

CHUMLEY. Wilson—this is a serious charge.

WILSON. Dr. Chumley, I've been with you for ten years. Are you gonna believe—what's your name again?

JUDGE. Gaffney. Judge Omar Gaffney.

WILSON. Thanks. You take the word of this old blister Gaffney ——

CHUMLEY. Wilson!

WILSON. Me! Me and a dame who sees a rabbit!

JUDGE. It's not Mrs. Simmons who sees a rabbit. It's her brother.

MYRTLE. Yes, it's Uncle Elwood.

JUDGE. If you'll come with me, Doctor ——

CHUMLEY. Very well, Judge. Wilson, I have a situation here. Wait for me. (HE *and* JUDGE *exit* R.)

WILSON. O K, Doctor. (MYRTLE MAE *is fascinated by* WILSON. *She lingers and looks at him.* HE *comes over to her, grinning.*)

WILSON. So your name's Myrtle Mae?

MYRTLE. What? Oh—yes —— (*She backs up.* HE *follows.*)

WILSON. If we grab your uncle you're liable to be comin' out to the sanitarium on visiting days?

MYRTLE. Oh, I don't really know—I ——

WILSON. Well, if you do, I'll be there.

MYRTLE. You will? Oh ——

WILSON. And if you don't see me right away—don't give up. Stick around. I'll show up.

MYRTLE. You will—? Oh ——

WILSON. Sure. (*He is still following her.*) You heard Dr. Chumley tell me to wait?

MYRTLE. Yeah ——

WILSON. Tell you what—while I'm waiting I sure could use a sandwich and a cup of coffee.

MYRTLE. Certainly. If you'll forgive me I'll precede you into the kitchen. (*She tries to go.* HE *traps her.*)

WILSON. Yessir—you're all right, Myrtle.

MYRTLE. What?

WILSON. Doctor Chumley noticed it right away. He don't miss a trick. (*Crowds closer; raises finger and pokes her arm for emphasis.*) Tell you somethin' else, Myrtle ——

MYRTLE. What?

WILSON. You not only got a nice build—but, kid, you got something else, too.

MYRTLE. What?

WILSON. You got the screwiest uncle that ever stuck his puss

inside our nuthouse. (MYRTLE *starts to exit in a huff, and* WIL-
SON *raises hand to give her a spank, but she turns and so he
puts up raised hand to his hair. They exit. The stage is
empty for a half second and then through* R. *comes* ELWOOD.
HE *comes in, goes to phone, dials a number.*)
ELWOOD. Hello, Chumley's Rest? Is Doctor Chumley there?
Oh—it's Mrs. Chumley! This is Elwood P. Dowd speaking.
How are you tonight? Tell me, Mrs. Chumley, were you able
to locate Harvey?—Don't worry about it. I'll find him. I'm
sorry I missed you at the McClure cocktail party. The people
were all charming and I was able to leave quite a few of my
cards. I waited until you phoned and said you couldn't come
because a patient had escaped. Where am I? I'm here. But
I'm leaving right away. I must find Harvey. Well, goodbye,
Mrs. Chumley. My regards to you and anybody else you happen to run into. Goodbye. (*Hangs up, then he sees the big
flat parcel against wall. He gets an "Ah, there it is!" expression on his face, goes over and takes off paper. We see revealed
a very strange thing. It is an oil painting of Elwood seated on
a chair while behind him stands a large white rabbit, in a
blue polka-dot collar and red necktie.* ELWOOD *holds it away
from him and surveys it proudly. Then looks around for a
place to put it. Takes it over and sets it on mantel. It obscures
the picture of Marcella Pinney Dowd completely. He gathers
up wrapping-paper, admires the rabbit again, tips his hat to
it and exits* R. *Phone rings and* VETA *enters* L., *followed by* DR.
CHUMLEY.)
VETA. Doctor, you might as well go home and wait. I'm suing
you for fifty thousand dollars and that's final. (*Crosses to
phone—her back is to mantel, she hasn't looked up.*)
CHUMLEY. (*Follows her to chair* L.) Mrs. Simmons ——
VETA. (*Into phone.*) Yes —— Well, all right.
CHUMLEY. This picture over your mantel.
VETA. That portrait happens to be the pride of this house.
CHUMLEY. (*Looking at her.*) Who painted it?
VETA. Oh, some man. I forget his name. He was around here
for the sittings, and then we paid him and he went away.
Hello—yes—No. This is Dexter 1567. (*Hangs up.*)
CHUMLEY. I suppose if you have the money to pay people, you
can persuade them to do anything.
VETA. Well, Dr. Chumley —— (*Walks over and faces him.*)

When you helped me out of that tub at your place, what did I say to you?

CHUMLEY. You expressed yourself. I don't remember the words.

VETA. I said, "Dr. Chumley, this is a belated civility." Isn't that what I said?

CHUMLEY. You said something of the sort ——

VETA. You brought this up; you may as well learn something quick. I took a course in art this last winter. The difference between a fine oil painting and a mechanical thing like a photograph is simply this: a photograph shows only the reality; a painting shows not only the reality but the dream behind it ——. It's our dreams that keep us going. That separate us from the beasts. I wouldn't even want to live if I thought it was all just eating and sleeping and taking off my clothes. Well—putting them on again —— (*Turns—sees picture—screams—totters—falls back.*) Oh—Doctor—oh—hold me—oh ——

CHUMLEY. (*Taking hold of her.*) Steady now—steady—don't get excited. Everything's all right. (*Seats her in chair L.*) Now —what's the matter?

VETA. (*Pointing.*) Doctor—that is *not* my mother!

CHUMLEY. I'm glad to hear that.

VETA. Oh, Doctor. Elwood's been here. He's been here.

CHUMLEY. Better be quiet. (*Phone rings.*) I'll take it. (*He answers it.*) Hello. Yes, yes—who's calling? (*Drops his hand over mouthpiece quickly.*) Here he is. Mrs. Simmons, it's your brother!

VETA. (*Getting up. Weak no longer.*) Oh—let me talk to him!

CHUMLEY. Don't tell him I'm here. Be casual.

VETA. Hello, Elwood—(*Laughs.*) Where are you? What? Oh—just a minute. (*Covers phone.*) He won't say where he is. He wants to know if Harvey is here.

CHUMLEY. Tell him Harvey *is* here.

VETA. But he isn't.

CHUMLEY. Tell him. That will bring him here, perhaps. Humor him. We have to humor them.

VETA. Yes—Elwood. Yes, dear. Harvey is here. Why don't you come home? Oh, oh, oh—well—all right. (*Looks around uncomfortably. Covers phone again.*) It won't work. He says for

44

me to call Harvey to the telephone.

CHUMLEY. Say Harvey is here, but can't come to the telephone. Say—he—say—he's in the bath-tub.

VETA. Bath-tub?

CHUMLEY. Say he's in the bath-tub, and you'll send him over there. That way we'll find out where he is.

VETA. Oh, Doctor!

CHUMLEY. Now, you've got to do it, Mrs. Simmons.

VETA. Hello, Elwood. Yes, dear. Harvey is here but he can't come to the telephone, he's in the bath-tub. I'll send him over as soon as he's dry. Where are you? Where, Elwood? (*Bangs phone.*)

CHUMLEY. Did he hang up?

VETA. Harvey just walked in the door! He told me to look in the bath-tub—it must be a stranger. But I know where he is. He's at Charlie's Place. That's a bar over at 12th and Main.

CHUMLEY. (*Picking up his hat from table* R.) 12th and Main. That's two blocks down and one over, isn't it?

VETA. Doctor—where are you going?

CHUMLEY. I'm going over there to get your brother and take him out to the sanitarium, where he belongs.

VETA. Oh, Dr. Chumley—don't do that. Send one of your attendants. I'm warning you.

CHUMLEY. But, Mrs. Simmons, if I am to help your brother ——

VETA. He can't be helped. (*Looks at picture.*) There is no help for him. He must be picked up and locked up and left.

CHUMLEY. You consider your brother a dangerous man?

VETA. Dangerous!

CHUMLEY. Why?

VETA. I won't tell you why, but if I didn't, why would I be asking for a permanent commitment for him?

CHUMLEY. Then I must observe this man. I must watch the expression on his face as he talks to this rabbit. He does talk to the rabbit, you say?

VETA. They tell each other everything.

CHUMLEY. What's that?

VETA. I said, of course he talks to him. But don't go after him, Doctor. You'll regret it if you do.

CHUMLEY. Nonsense—(*He is going toward* R.) You underestimate me, Mrs. Simmons.

VETA. Oh, no, Doctor. You underestimate my brother.

CHUMLEY. Not at all. Don't worry now. I can handle him!
(*He exits R.*)

VETA. (*After he has gone.*) You can handle him? That's what
you think! (*Calls up* L.) Myrtle Mae! See who's in the bath-
tub. OH!

CURTAIN

ACT II

SCENE 2

SCENE: *The main office at* CHUMLEY'S REST *again.*
TIME: *Four hours after the curtain of Scene 1, Act II.*
AT RISE. KELLY *is on the phone.* WILSON *is helping* SAN-
DERSON *carry boxes of books out of his office up* L. *and
onto table* C.

KELLY. Thank you. I may call later. (*Hangs up.*)

WILSON. (L. *of table* R.) How about the stuff in your room,
Doctor—upstairs?

SANDERSON. (*To table, puts box on it.*) All packed—thanks—
Wilson.

WILSON. Tough your gettin' bounced. I had you pegged for
the one who'd make the grade.

SANDERSON. Those are the breaks.

WILSON. When you takin' off?

SANDERSON. As soon as Dr. Chumley gets back.

WILSON. (*To* KELLY.) Did you get a report back yet from the
desk sergeant in the police accident bureau?

KELLY. Not yet. I just talked to the downtown dispensary.
They haven't seen him.

WILSON. It's beginning to smell awful funny to me. Four
hours he's been gone and not a word from him. (*Goes to*
SANDERSON—*extends hand.*) I may not see you again, Doctor,
so I want to say I wish you a lot of luck and I'm mighty
sorry you got a kick in the atpray.

SANDERSON. Thanks, Wilson—good luck to you, too—

46

WILSON. (*Starts to exit, but stops at door back c., turns toward* KELLY.) Look, Kelly, let me know when you hear from the desk sergeant again. If there's no sign of the doctor, I'm goin' into town and look for him. He should know better'n to go after a psycho without me. (*Starts up c.*)

SANDERSON. I'd like to help look for the doctor, too, Wilson.

WILSON. That's swell of you, Doctor, right after he give you the brush.

SANDERSON. I've no resentment against Dr. Chumley. He was right. I was wrong. (*He rises.*) Chumley is the biggest man in his field. It's my loss not to be able to work with him. (*Crosses up to bookcase.*)

WILSON. You're not so small yourself, Doctor ——

SANDERSON. Thanks, Wilson.

WILSON. Don't mention it. (*Exits* U.C.)

KELLY. (*Taking deep breath and standing above desk.*) Dr. Sanderson ——

SANDERSON. (*Without looking up.*) Yes ——

KELLY. (*Plunging in.*) Well, Doctor —— (*Takes another deep breath.*) I'd like to say that *I* wish you a lot of luck, too, and I'm sorry to see you leave.

SANDERSON. (*Going on with his work.*) Are you sure you can spare these good wishes, Miss Kelly?

KELLY. (*She flushes.*) On second thought—I guess I can't. Forget it. (*Starts for below desk.*)

SANDERSON. (*Now looking up.*) Miss Kelly —— (*To back of table.*) This is for nothing—just a little advice. I'd be a little careful if I were you about the kind of company I kept.

KELLY. I beg your pardon, Doctor?

SANDERSON. (*Crosses c.*) You don't have to. I told you it was free. I saw you Saturday night—dancing with that drip in the Rose Room down at the Frontier Hotel.

KELLY. (*Putting books on desk.*) Oh, did you? I didn't notice you.

SANDERSON. I'd be a little careful of him, Kelly. He looked to me like a schizophrenic all the way across the floor.

KELLY. You really shouldn't have given him a thought, Doctor. He was my date—not yours. (*Hands book to* SANDERSON.)

SANDERSON. That was his mentality. The rest of him—well —— (*Puts book in box front of table.*)

47

KELLY. But she was beautiful, though—

SANDERSON. Who?

KELLY. That girl you were with—

SANDERSON. I thought you didn't notice?

KELLY. You bumped into us twice. How could I help it?

SANDERSON. Not that it makes any difference to you, but that girl is a charming little lady. *She* has a sweet kind disposition and *she* knows how to conduct herself.

KELLY. Funny she couldn't rate a better date on a Saturday night!

SANDERSON. And she has an excellent mind.

KELLY. Why doesn't she use it?

SANDERSON. (*Crossing toward* KELLY.) Oh, I don't suppose you're to be censured for the flippant hard shell you have. You're probably compensating for something.

KELLY. I am not, and don't you use any of your psychiatry on me.

SANDERSON. Oh—if I could try something else on you—just once! Just to see if you'd melt under any circumstances. I doubt it.

KELLY. You'll never know, Doctor.

SANDERSON. Because you interest me as a case history—that's all. I'd like to know where you get that inflated ego— (*Goes back of desk.*)

KELLY. (*Now close to tears.*) If you aren't the meanest person —inflated ego—case history! (*Turns and starts out* C.)

SANDERSON. Don't run away. Let's finish it. (PHONE *rings.*)

KELLY. Oh, leave me alone. (*Goes to answer it.*)

SANDERSON. Gladly. (*Exits.*)

KELLY. (*In angry, loud voice.*) Chumley's Rest. Yes—Sergeant. No accident report on him either in town or the suburbs. Look, Sergeant—maybe we better—(*Looks up as door down* L. *opens and* ELWOOD *enters. He is carrying a bouquet of dahlias.*) Oh, never mind, Sergeant. They're here now. (*Hangs up. Goes toward* ELWOOD.) Mr. Dowd—!

ELWOOD. (*Crosses to* C. *Handing her flowers.*) Good evening, my dear. These are for you.

KELLY. (*Crosses to* C.) For me—oh, thank you!

ELWOOD. They're quite fresh, too. I just picked them outside.

48

KELLY. I hope Dr. Chumley didn't see you. They're his prize dahlias. Did he go upstairs? (*Backing up.*)

ELWOOD. Not knowing, I cannot state. Those colors are lovely against your hair.

KELLY. I've never worn burnt orange. It's such a trying color.

ELWOOD. You would improve any color, my dear.

KELLY. Thank you. Did Dr. Chumley go over to his house?

ELWOOD. I don't know. Where is Dr. Sanderson?

KELLY. In his office there—I think. (*Crosses back to desk.*)

ELWOOD. (*Going over to door and knocking.*) Thank you.

SANDERSON. (*Enters.*) Dowd! There you are!

ELWOOD. I have a cab outside, if it's possible for you and Miss Kelly to get away now.

SANDERSON. Where is Dr. Chumley?

ELWOOD. Is he coming with us? That's nice.

KELLY. (*Answering question on* SANDERSON'S *face.*) I don't know, Doctor.

ELWOOD. I must apologize for being a few seconds late. I thought Miss Kelly should have some flowers. (*Crosses to table.*) After what happened out here this afternoon the flowers really should be from you, Doctor. As you grow older and pretty women pass you by, you will think with deep gratitude of these generous girls of your youth. Shall we go now? (KELLY *exits.*)

SANDERSON. (*Pressing buzzer.*) Just a moment, Dowd —— (*Starts* R.) The situation has changed since we met this afternoon. But I urge you to have no resentments. Dr. Chumley is your friend. He only wants to help you.

ELWOOD. That's very nice of him. I would like to help him, too. (*At table.*)

SANDERSON. If you'll begin by taking a cooperative attitude —that's half the battle. We all have to face reality, Dowd— sooner or later.

ELWOOD. Doctor, I wrestled with reality for forty years, and I am happy to state that I finally won out over it. (KELLY *enters.*) Won't you and Miss Kelly join me—down at Charlie's? (*Enter* WILSON *from* C.)

WILSON. Here you are! (*Goes over to* ELWOOD.) Upstairs, buddy—we're going upstairs. Is the doctor O.K.? (*He asks*

ELWOOD. There must be some mistake. Miss Kelly and Dr. Sanderson and I are going down-town for a drink. I'd be glad to have you come with us, Mr. ——

WILSON. Wilson.

ELWOOD. —Wilson. They have a wonderful floor show.

WILSON. Yeah? Well—wait'll you see the floor show we've got —— Upstairs, buddy!

SANDERSON. Just a minute, Wilson. Where did you say Dr. Chumley went, Dowd?

ELWOOD. As I said, he did not confide his plans in me.

WILSON. You mean the doctor ain't showed up yet? (*Crosses to desk*.)

KELLY. Not yet.

WILSON. Where is he?

SANDERSON. That's what we're trying to find out.

KELLY. Mr. Dowd walked in here by himself.

WILSON. Oh, he did, eh? Listen, you—talk fast or I'm workin' you over!

ELWOOD. I'd rather you didn't do that, and I'd rather you didn't even mention such a thing in the presence of a lovely young lady like Miss Kelly—

SANDERSON. Mr. Dowd, Dr. Chumley went into town to pick you up. That was four hours ago.

ELWOOD. Where has the evening gone to?

WILSON. Listen to that! Smart, eh?

SANDERSON. Just a minute, Wilson. Did you see Dr. Chumley tonight, Dowd?

ELWOOD. Yes, I did. He came into Charlie's Place at dinner-time. It is a cozy spot. Let's all go there and talk it over with a tall one.

WILSON. We're going no place—(*Crosses between* ELWOOD *and* SANDERSON.) Now I'm askin' you a question, and if you don't button up your lip and give me some straight answers I'm gonna beat it out of you!

ELWOOD. What you suggest is impossible.

WILSON. What's that?

ELWOOD. You suggest that I button up my lip and give you some straight answers. It can't be done. (*Sits chair* L. *of table*.)

SANDERSON. Let me handle this, Wilson. (*Puts* WILSON *to* L.)
WILSON. Well, handle it, then. But find out where the Doctor is. (*Back of desk.*)
SANDERSON. Dr. Chumley *did* come into Charlie's Place, you say?
ELWOOD. He did, and I was very glad to see him.
WILSON. Go on ——
ELWOOD. He had asked for me, and naturally the proprietor brought him over and left him. We exchanged the conventional greetings. I said, "How do you do, Dr. Chumley," and he said, "How do you do, Mr. Dowd." I believe we said that at least once.
WILSON. Okay—okay—
ELWOOD. I am trying to be factual. I then introduced him to Harvey.
WILSON. To who?
KELLY. A white rabbit. Six feet tall.
WILSON. Six feet!
ELWOOD. Six feet one and a half!
WILSON. Okay—fool around with him, and the Doctor is probably some place bleedin' to death in a ditch.
ELWOOD. If those were his plans for the evening he did not tell me.
SANDERSON. Go on, Dowd.
ELWOOD. Dr. Chumley sat down in the booth with us. I was sitting on the outside like this. (*Shows.*) Harvey was on the inside near the wall, and Dr. Chumley was seated directly across from Harvey where he could look at him.
WILSON. (*Crosses a step* R.) That's right. Spend all night on the seatin' arrangements!
ELWOOD. Harvey then suggested that I buy him a drink. Knowing that he does not like to drink alone, I suggested to Dr. Chumley that we join him.
WILSON. And so?
ELWOOD. We joined him.
WILSON. Go on—go on.
ELWOOD. We joined him again.
WILSON. Then what?
ELWOOD. We kept right on joining him.
WILSON. Oh, skip all the joining!

ELWOOD. You are asking me to skip a large portion of the evening—

WILSON. Tell us what happened—come on—please ——

ELWOOD. Dr. Chumley and Harvey got into a conversation —quietly at first. Later it became rather heated and Dr. Chumley raised his voice.

WILSON. Yeah—why?

ELWOOD. Harvey seemed to feel that Dr. Chumley should assume part of the financial responsibility of the joining, but Dr. Chumley didn't seem to want to do that.

KELLY. (It breaks out from her.) I can believe that part of it!

WILSON. Let him talk. See how far he'll go. This guy's got guts.

ELWOOD. I agreed to take the whole thing because I did not want any trouble. We go down to Charlie's quite often—Harvey and I—and the proprietor is a fine man with an interesting approach to life. Then the other matter came up.

WILSON. Cut the damned double-talk and get on with it!

ELWOOD. Mr. Wilson, you are a sincere type of person, but I must ask you not to use that language in the presence of Miss Kelly. (He makes a short bow to her.)

SANDERSON. You're right, Dowd, and we're sorry. You say—the other matter came up?

ELWOOD. There was a beautiful blonde woman—a Mrs. Smethills—and her escort seated in the booth across from us. Dr. Chumley went over to sit next to her, explaining to her that they had once met. In Chicago. Her escort escorted Dr. Chumley back to me and Harvey and tried to point out that it would be better for Dr. Chumley to mind his own affairs. Does he have any?

WILSON. Does he have any what?

ELWOOD. Does he have any affairs?

WILSON. How would I know?

KELLY. Please hurry, Mr. Dowd—we're all so worried.

ELWOOD. Dr. Chumley then urged Harvey to go with him over to Blondie's Chicken Inn. Harvey wanted to go to Eddie's instead. While they were arguing about it I went to the bar to order another drink, and when I came back they were gone.

WILSON. Where did they go? I mean where did the Doctor go?

ELWOOD. I don't know—I had a date out here with Dr. Sanderson and Miss Kelly, and I came out to pick them up—hoping that later on we might run into Harvey and the Doctor and make a party of it.

WILSON. So—you satisfied? You got his story—(*Goes over to* ELWOOD, *fists clenched.*) O.K. You're lyin' and we know it!

ELWOOD. I never lie, Mr. Wilson.

WILSON. You've done somethin' with the Doctor and I'm findin' out what it is ——

SANDERSON. (*Moving after* him.) Don't touch him, Wilson ——

KELLY. Maybe he isn't lying, Wilson—

WILSON. (*Turning on them. Furiously.*) That's all this guy is, is a bunch of lies! You two don't believe this story he tells about the Doctor sittin' there talkin' to a big white rabbit, do you?

KELLY. Maybe Dr. Chumley *did* go to Charlie's Place.

WILSON. And saw a big rabbit, I suppose.

ELWOOD. And why not? Harvey was there. At first the Doctor seemed a little frightened of Harvey but that gave way to admiration as the evening wore on—. The evening wore on! That's a nice expression. With your permission I'll say it again. The evening wore on.

WILSON. (*Lunging at him.*) With your permission I'm gonna knock your teeth down your throat!

ELWOOD. (*Not moving an inch.*) Mr. Wilson—haven't you some old friends you can go play with? (SANDERSON *has grabbed* WILSON *and is struggling with him.*)

WILSON. (*He is being held. Glares fiercely at* ELWOOD. KELLY *dials phone.*) The nerve of this guy! He couldn't come out here with an ordinary case of D.T.'s. No. He has to come out with a six-foot rabbit.

ELWOOD. (*Rises—goes toward desk* L.) Stimulating as all this is, I really must be getting down-town.

KELLY. (*On phone.*) Charlie's Place? Is Dr. Chumley anywhere around there? He was there with Mr. Dowd earlier in the evening. What? Well, don't bite my head off! (*Hangs up.*) My, that man was mad. He said Mr. Dowd was welcome any time, but his friend was not.

ELWOOD. That's Mr. McNulty the bartender. He thinks a lot of me. Now let's all go down and have a drink.

WILSON. Wait a minute ——

KELLY. Mr. Dowd ——(*Goes over to him.*)

ELWOOD. Yes, my dear—may I hold your hand?

KELLY. Yes—if you want to. (ELWOOD *does.*) Poor Mrs. Chumley is so worried. Something must have happened to the Doctor. Won't you please try and remember something—something else that might help her? Please ——

ELWOOD. For you I would do anything. I would almost be willing to live my life over again. Almost. But I've told it all.

KELLY. You're sure?

ELWOOD. Quite sure—but ask me again, anyway, won't you? I liked that warm tone you had in your voice just then.

SANDERSON. (*Without realizing he is saying it.*) So did I. (*Looks at* KELLY.)

WILSON. Oh, nuts!

ELWOOD. What?

WILSON. Nuts!

ELWOOD. Oh! I must be going. I have things to do.

KELLY. Mr. Dowd, what is it you do?

ELWOOD. (*Sits, as* KELLY *sits* R. *of desk.*) Harvey and I sit in the bars and we have a drink or two and play the juke-box. Soon the faces of the other people turn toward mine and smile. They are saying: "We don't know your name, Mister, but you're a lovely fellow." Harvey and I warm ourselves in all these golden moments. We have entered as strangers—soon we have friends. They come over. They sit with us. They drink with us. They talk to us. They tell about the big terrible things they have done. The big wonderful things they *will* do. Their hopes, their regrets, their loves, their hates. All very large because nobody ever brings anything small into a bar. Then I introduce them to Harvey. And he is bigger and grander than anything they offer me. When they leave, they leave impressed. The same people seldom come back—but that's envy, my dear. There's a little bit of envy in the best of us—too bad, isn't it?

SANDERSON. (*Leaning forward.*) How did you happen to call him Harvey?

ELWOOD. Harvey is his name.

SANDERSON. How do you know that?

ELWOOD. That was rather an interesting coincidence, Doctor. One night several years ago I was walking early in the evening along Fairfax Street—between 18th and 19th. You know that block?

SANDERSON. Yes, yes.

ELWOOD. I had just helped Ed Hickey into a taxi. Ed had been mixing his rye with his gin, and I felt he needed conveying. I started to walk down the street when I heard a voice saying: "Good evening, Mr. Dowd." I turned and there was this great white rabbit leaning against a lamp-post. Well, I thought nothing of that, because when you have lived in a town as long as I have lived in this one, you get used to the fact that everybody knows your name. Naturally, I went over to chat with him. He said to me: "Ed Hickey is a little spiffed this evening, or could I be mistaken?" Well, of course he was not mistaken. I think the world and all of Ed but he was spiffed. Well, anyway, we stood there and talked, and finally I said—"You have the advantage of me. You know my name and I don't know yours." Right back at me he said: "What name do you like?" Well, I didn't even have to think a minute: Harvey has always been my favorite name. So I said, "Harvey," and this is the interesting part of the whole thing. He said—"What a coincidence! My name happens to be Harvey."

SANDERSON. (*Crossing above desk.*) What was your father's name, Dowd?

ELWOOD. John. John Frederick.

SANDERSON. Dowd, when you were a child you had a play mate, didn't you? Someone you were very fond of—with whom you spent many happy, carefree hours?

ELWOOD. Oh, yes, Doctor. Didn't you?

SANDERSON. What was his name?

ELWOOD. Verne. Verne McElhinney. Did you ever know the McElhinneys, Doctor?

SANDERSON. No.

ELWOOD. Too bad. There were a lot of them, and they circulated. Wonderful people.

SANDERSON. Think carefully, Dowd. Wasn't there someone, somewhere, some time, whom you knew—by the name of Harvey? Didn't you ever know anybody by that name?

ELWOOD. No, Doctor. No one. Maybe that's why I always

had such hopes for it.

SANDERSON. Come on, Wilson, we'll take Mr. Dowd upstairs now.

WILSON. I'm taking him nowhere. You've made this your show —now run it. Lettin' him sit here—forgettin' all about Dr. Chumley! O.K. It's your show—you run it.

SANDERSON. Come on, Dowd— (*Pause. Putting out his hand.*) Come on, Elwood—

ELWOOD. (*Rises.*) Very well, Lyman. (SANDERSON *and* KELLY *take him to door.*) But I'm afraid I won't be able to visit with you for long. I have promised Harvey I will take him to the floor-show. (THEY *exit* U.C.) (WILSON *is alone. Sits at desk, looks at his watch.*)

WILSON. Oh, boy! (*Puts head in arms on desk.*) (DR. CHUMLEY *enters* L. WILSON *does not see him until he gets almost* C. *stage.*)

WILSON. (*Jumping up, going to him.*) Dr. Chumley—Are you all right?

CHUMLEY. All right? Of course I'm all right. I'm being followed. Lock that door.

WILSON. (*Goes to door* L., *locks it.*) Who's following you?

CHUMLEY. None of your business. (*Exits into office* R., *locks door behind him.*) (WILSON *stands a moment perplexed, then shrugs shoulders, turns off lights and exits* U.C. *The stage is dimly lit. Then from door* L. *comes the rattle of the doorknob. Door opens and shuts, and we hear locks opening and closing, and see light from hall on stage. The invisible Harvey has come in. There is a count of eight while he crosses the stage, then door of* CHUMLEY's *office opens and closes, with sound of locks clicking. Harvey has gone in—and then ——*

CURTAIN

ACT III

SCENE: *The sanitarium office at Chumley's Rest.*
TIME: *A few minutes after the curtain of Act II.*
AT RISE: *Lights are still dim as at preceding curtain. There is a loud knocking at L. and the sound of* CHUMLEY'S *voice calling,* "Wilson! Wilson!"

WILSON. (*Enters from* C., *opens door* L. CHUMLEY *enters, white-faced.*) How didja get out here, Doctor? I just saw you go in there.
CHUMLEY. I went out through my window. Wilson—don't leave me!
WILSON. No, Doctor.
CHUMLEY. Get that man Dowd out of here.
WILSON. Yes, Doctor. (*Starts to exit* C.)
CHUMLEY. No—don't leave me!
WILSON. (*Turning back—confused.*) But you said—
CHUMLEY. Dumphy—on the telephone.
WILSON. Yes, Doctor. (*Crosses to phone.*) Dumphy—give that guy Dowd his clothes and get him down here right away. (*A knock on the door.*)
CHUMLEY. Don't leave me!
WILSON. Just a minute, Doctor. (*Crosses up and turns on lights. Crosses down and opens door* L.) Judge Gaffney.
JUDGE. I want to see Dr. Chumley. (*Enter* JUDGE *and* MYRTLE MAE.)
WILSON. Hiya, Myrtle.
MYRTLE. Hello.
JUDGE. Chumley, we've got to talk to you. This thing is serious.
MYRTLE. It certainly is.
GAFFNEY. More serious than you suspect. Where can we go to talk? (*Moves toward Chumley's office.*)
CHUMLEY. (*Blocking door.*) Not in there.

57

WILSON. The Doctor doesn't want you in his office.

DR. CHUMLEY. No, sir.

JUDGE. Then sit down, Dr. Chumley. Sit down, Myrtle Mae.

CHUMLEY. *(Dazed.)* Sit down, Dr. Chumley. Sit down, Myrtle Mae. Don't go, Wilson. Don't leave me.

JUDGE. Now, Chumley, here are my notes—the facts. Can anybody hear me?

WILSON. Yeah, we can all hear you. Is that good?

JUDGE. *(Gives Wilson a look of reproof.)* Now, Chumley, has it ever occurred to you that possibly there might *be* something like this rabbit Harvey?

MYRTLE. Of course there isn't. And anybody who thinks so is crazy. (CHUMLEY *stares at her.*) Well, don't look at me like that. There's nothing funny about me. I'm like my father's family—they're all dead.

JUDGE. Now, then, my client, the plaintiff, Mrs. Veta Louise Simmons, under oath, swears that on the morning of November 2nd while standing in the kitchen of her home, hearing her name called, she turned and saw this great white rabbit, Harvey. He was staring at her. Resenting the intrusion, the plaintiff made certain remarks and drove the creature from the room. He went.

CHUMLEY. What did she say to him?

JUDGE. She was emphatic. The remarks are not important.

CHUMLEY. I want to know how she got this creature out of her sanitarium—I mean—her home.

MYRTLE. I hate to have you tell him, Judge. It isn't a bit like Mother.

WILSON. Quit stalling. Let's have it.

GAFFNEY. She looked him right in the eye and exclaimed in the heat of anger—"To hell with you!"

CHUMLEY. *(Looking at door.)* "To hell with you!" He left?

JUDGE. Yes, he left. But that's beside the point. The point is —is it perjury or is it something we can cope with? I ask for your opinion. (KELLY *enters from stairs* U.C. SANDERSON *comes from* U.C. *diet kitchen.*)

SANDERSON. Ruthie! I've been looking all over for you.

CHUMLEY. Dr. Sanderson, disregard what I said this afternoon. I want you on my staff. You are a very astute young man.

KELLY. Oh, Lyman! Did you hear?

SANDERSON. Oh, baby!

KELLY. See you later. (*Exits* U.C., *blowing him a kiss.* SANDERSON *exits into his office.*)

MYRTLE. You've just got to keep Uncle Elwood out here, Doctor. (JUDGE *crosses to desk.*)

CHUMLEY. No. I want this sanitarium the way it was before that man came out here this afternoon.

MYRTLE. I know what you mean.

CHUMLEY. You do?

MYRTLE. Well, it certainly gets on anyone's nerves the way Uncle Elwood knows what's going to happen before it happens. This morning, for instance, he told us that Harvey told him Mrs. McElhinney's Aunt Rose would drop in on her unexpectedly tonight from Cleveland.

CHUMLEY. And did she?

MYRTLE. Did she what?

CHUMLEY. Aunt Rose—did she come just as Harvey said she would?

MYRTLE. Oh, yes. Those things always turn out the way Uncle Elwood says they will—but what of it? What do we care about the McElhinneys?

CHUMLEY. You say this sort of thing happens often?

MYRTLE. Yes, and isn't it silly? Uncle Elwood says Harvey tells him everything. Harvey knows everything. How could he when there is no such thing as Harvey?

CHUMLEY. (*Goes over, tries lock at door* R.) Fly-specks. I've been spending my life among fly-specks while miracles have been leaning on lamp-posts on 18th and Fairfax.

VETA. (*Enters down* L. *Looks around cautiously. Sighs with relief.*) Good. Nobody here but people.

MYRTLE. Oh, Mother! You promised you wouldn't come out here.

VETA. Well, good evening. Now, Myrtle Mae, I brought Elwood's bathrobe. Well, why are you all just sitting here? I thought you'd be committing him.

JUDGE. Sit down there, girl. (*Motioning to chair near Wilson.*)

VETA. I will not sit down there. (*Sits chair* R. *of desk.*)

WILSON. How about you and me stepping out Saturday night,

Myrtle Mae?

VETA. Certainly not. Myrtle Mae, come here.

MYRTLE. I'm sorry. (*Goes down to* Veta.)

VETA. Is everything settled?

CHUMLEY. It will be.

SANDERSON. (*Enters from his office.*) Doctor, may I give an opinion?

CHUMLEY. Yes, do. By all means.

VETA. (*Sniffing.*) His opinion! Omar—he's the doctor I told you about. The eyes!

SANDERSON. It's my opinion that Elwood P. Dowd is suffering from a third-degree hallucination and the—(*Pointing at Veta's back.*) other party concerned is the victim of auto-suggestion. I recommend shock formula number 977 for him and bed-rest at home for—(*Points again.*)

CHUMLEY. You do?

SANDERSON. That's my diagnosis, Doctor. (*To Veta.*) Mr. Dowd will not see this rabbit any more after this injection. We've used it in hundreds of psychopathic cases.

VETA. Don't you call my brother a psychopathic case! There's never been anything like that in our family.

MYRTLE. If you didn't think Uncle Elwood was psychopathic, why did you bring him out here?

VETA. Where else could I take him, I couldn't take him to jail, could I? Besides, this is not your uncle's fault. Why did Harvey have to speak to him in the first place? With the town full of people, why did he have to bother Elwood?

JUDGE. Stop putting your oar in. Keep your oar out. If this shock formula brings people back to reality, give it to him. That's where we want Elwood.

CHUMLEY. I'm not sure that it would work in a case of this kind, Doctor.

SANDERSON. It always has.

VETA. Harvey always follows Elwood home.

CHUMLEY. He does?

VETA. Yes. But if you give him the formula and Elwood doesn't see Harvey, he won't let him in. Then when he comes to the door, I'll deal with him.

MYRTLE. Mother, won't you stop talking about Harvey as if there was such a thing?

VETA. Myrtle Mae, you've got a lot to learn and I hope you never learn it. (*She starts up toward* Wilson.) (ELWOOD *is heard off stage humming.*)

JUDGE. Sh! Here he is.

ELWOOD. (*Enters* C.) Good evening, everybody. (ALL *nod.*)

VETA. Good evening, Elwood. I've brought you your bathrobe.

ELWOOD. Thank you, Veta.

JUDGE. Well, Chumley, what do we do? We've got to do something.

VETA. Oh, yes, we must.

MYRTLE. I should say so.

CHUMLEY. (*Looking at door.*) Yes, it's imperative.

ELWOOD. Well, while you're making up your minds, why don't we all go down to Charlie's and have a drink?

VETA. You're not going anywhere, Elwood. You're staying here.

MYRTLE. Yes, Uncle Elwood.

JUDGE. Stay here, son.

ELWOOD. I plan to leave. You want me to stay. An element of conflict in any discussion is a good thing. It means everybody is taking part and nobody is left out. I like that. Oh—how did you get along with Harvey, Doctor?

CHUMLEY. Sh-h!

JUDGE. We're waiting for your answer, Doctor.

CHUMLEY. What?

JUDGE. What is your decision?

CHUMLEY. I must be alone with this man. Will you all step into the other room? (MYRTLE *exits* U.L.) I'll have my diagnosis in a moment.

VETA. Do hurry, Doctor.

CHUMLEY. I will.

VETA. You stay here, Elwood. (*She and* JUDGE GAFFNEY *exit* U.L.)

CHUMLEY. Here, Mr. Dowd. Let me give you this chair. (*Indicates chair* L. *of table* R.) Let me give you a cigar. (*Does so.*) Is there anything else I can get you?

ELWOOD. (*Seated in chair.*) What did you have in mind?

CHUMLEY. Mr. Dowd—(*Lowers voice, looks toward office.*) What kind of a man are you? Where do you come from?

ELWOOD. (*Getting out card.*) Didn't I give you one of my cards?

CHUMLEY. And where on the face of this tired old earth did you find a thing like him?

ELWOOD. Harvey the Pooka?

CHUMLEY. (*Sits chair R. of table.*) Is it true that he has a function—that he —— ?

ELWOOD. Gets advance notice? I'm happy to say it is. Harvey is versatile. Harvey can stop clocks.

DR. CHUMLEY. What?

ELWOOD. You've heard that expression, "His face would stop a clock"?

CHUMLEY. Yes. But why? To what purpose?

ELWOOD. Harvey says that he can look at your clock and stop it and you can go away as long as you like with whomever you like and go as far as you like. And when you come back not one minute will have ticked by.

CHUMLEY. You mean that he actually —— ? (*Looks toward office.*)

ELWOOD. Einstein has overcome time and space. Harvey has overcome not only time and space—but any objections.

CHUMLEY. And does he do this for you?

ELWOOD. He is willing to at any time, but so far I've never been able to think of any place I'd rather be. I always have a wonderful time just where I am, whomever I'm with. I'm having a fine time right now with you, Doctor. (*Holds up cigar.*) Corona-Corona.

CHUMLEY. I know where I'd go.

ELWOOD. Where?

CHUMLEY. I'd go to Akron.

ELWOOD. Akron?

CHUMLEY. There's a cottage camp outside Akron in a grove of maple trees, cool, green, beautiful.

ELWOOD. My favorite tree.

CHUMLEY. I would go there with a pretty young woman, a strange woman, a quiet woman.

ELWOOD. Under a tree?

CHUMLEY. I wouldn't even want to know her name. I would be—just Mr. Brown.

ELWOOD. Why wouldn't you want to know her name? You

62

might be acquainted with the same people.

CHUMLEY. I would send out for cold beer. I would talk to her. I would tell her things I have never told anyone—things that are locked in here. (*Beats his breast.* ELWOOD *looks over at his chest with interest.*) And then I would send out for more cold beer.

ELWOOD. No whiskey?

CHUMLEY. Beer is better.

ELWOOD. Maybe under a tree. But she might like a highball.

CHUMLEY. I wouldn't let her talk to me, but as I talked I would want her to reach out a soft white hand and stroke my head and say, "Poor thing! Oh, you poor, poor thing!"

ELWOOD. How long would you like that to go on?

CHUMLEY. Two weeks.

ELWOOD. Wouldn't that get monotonous? Just Akron, beer, and "poor, poor thing" for two weeks?

CHUMLEY. No. No, it would not. It would be wonderful.

ELWOOD. I can't help but feel you're making a mistake in not allowing that woman to talk. If she gets around at all, she may have picked up some very interesting little news items. And I'm sure you're making a mistake with all that beer and no whiskey. But it's your two weeks.

CHUMLEY. (*Dreamily.*) Cold beer at Akron and one last fling! God, man!

ELWOOD. Do you think you'd like to lie down for awhile?

CHUMLEY. No. No. Tell me Mr. Dowd, could he—would he do this for me?

ELWOOD. He could and he might. I have never heard Harvey say a word against Akron. By the way, Doctor, where is Harvey?

CHUMLEY, (*Rising. Very cautiously.*) Why, don't you know?

ELWOOD. The last time I saw him he was with you.

CHUMLEY. Ah!

ELWOOD. Oh! He's probably waiting for me down at Charlie's.

CHUMLEY. (*With a look of cunning toward his office.*) That's it! He's down at Charlie's.

ELWOOD. Excuse me, Doctor. (*Rises, starts upstage.*)

CHUMLEY. (*Going* U.L. *of table.*) No, no Mr. Dowd. Not in there.

ELWOOD. I couldn't leave without saying good-night to my

friend, Dr. Sanderson

CHUMLEY. Mr. Dowd, Dr. Sanderson is not your friend. None of those people are your friends. *I* am your friend.

ELWOOD. Thank you, Doctor. And I'm yours.

CHUMLEY. And this sister of yours—she is at the bottom of this conspiracy against you. She's trying to persuade me to lock you up. Today she had commitment papers drawn up. She's got your power of attorney and the key to your safety box. She brought you out here ——

ELWOOD. My sister did all that in one afternoon? Veta is certainly a whirlwind.

CHUMLEY. (*Moving down below desk.*) God, man, haven't you any righteous indignation?

ELWOOD. Dr. Chumley, my mother used to say to me, "In this world, Elwood"—she always called me Elwood—she'd say, "In this world, Elwood, you must be oh, so smart or oh, so pleasant." For years I was smart. I recommend pleasant. You may quote me.

CHUMLEY. Just the same, I will protect you if I have to commit her. Would you like me to do that?

ELWOOD. No, Doctor, not unless Veta wanted it that way. Oh, not that you don't have a nice place out here, but I think Veta would be happier at home with me and Harvey and Myrtle Mae. (KELLY *enters from* C. *with flower in hair, goes to put magazines on table* R. ELWOOD *turns to her.*) Miss Kelly! "Diviner grace has never brightened this enchanting face!" (*To Chumley.*) Ovid's Fifth Elegy. (*To Miss Kelly.*) My dear, you will never look lovelier!

KELLY. I'll never feel happier, Mr. Dowd. I know it. (*Kisses him.*)

CHUMLEY. Well!

KELLY. Yes, Doctor. (*Exits up stairs* C.) (WILSON *enters hall in time to see the kiss.*)

ELWOOD. I wonder if I would be able to remember any more of that poem?

WILSON. Say, maybe this rabbit gag is a good one. Kelly never kissed me.

ELWOOD. (*Looking at* Wilson.) Ovid has always been my favorite poet.

WILSON. O.K., pal—You're discharged. This way out—(*Takes him by arm down stage.*)

64

CHUMLEY. Wilson! Take your hands off that man!

WILSON. (R. *of desk*.) What?

CHUMLEY. Apologize to Mr. Dowd.

WILSON. Apologize to him—this guy with the rabbit? (*He is below desk*.)

CHUMLEY. (*Looking toward his office*.) Apologize! Apologize ——

WILSON. I apologize. This is the door.

ELWOOD. If I leave, I'll remember. (WILSON *exits* D.L.)

CHUMLEY. Wait a minute, Dowd. Do women often come up to you and kiss you like Miss Kelly did just now?

ELWOOD. Every once in a while.

CHUMLEY. Yes?

ELWOOD. I encourage it, too.

CHUMLEY. (*To himself*.) To hell with decency! I've got to have that rabbit! Go ahead and knock. (ELWOOD *starts for Sanderson's door just as* SANDERSON *comes out*.)

ELWOOD. Dr. Sanderson, I couldn't leave without ——

SANDERSON. Just a minute, Dowd—(*To Chumley*.) Doctor, do you agree with my diagnosis?

CHUMLEY. Yes, yes! Call them all in.

SANDERSON. Thank you, Doctor. Mrs. Simmons—Judge Gaffney—will you step in here for a minute, please?

VETA. (*Enters*.) Is it settled? (MYRTLE *and* JUDGE *enter*.)

CHUMLEY. I find I concur with Dr. Sanderson!

SANDERSON. Thank you, Doctor.

MYRTLE. Oh, that's wonderful! What a relief!

JUDGE. Good boy!

ELWOOD. Well, let's celebrate—(*Takes little book out of his pocket*.) I've got some new bars listed in the back of this book.

CHUMLEY. (*Speaking to others in low tone*.) This injection carries a violent reaction. We can't give it to him without his consent. Will he give it?

VETA. Of course he will, if I ask him.

CHUMLEY. To give up this rabbit—I doubt it.

MYRTLE. Don't ask him. Just give it to him.

ELWOOD. "Bessie's Barn Dance. Blondie's Chicken Inn. Better Late Than Never—Bennie's Drive In" ——

VETA. Elwood!

ELWOOD. We'll go to Bennie's Drive In—. We should telephone for a table. How many of us will there be, Veta?

VETA. (*Starting to count, then catching herself.*) Oh—Elwood!

CHUMLEY. Mr. Dowd, I have a formula—977—that will be
good for you. Will you take it?

JUDGE. Elwood, you won't see this rabbit any more.

SANDERSON. But you will see your responsibilities, your duties
——

ELWOOD. I'm sure if you thought of it, Doctor, it must be a
very fine thing. And if I happen to run into anyone who
needs it, I'll be glad to recommend it. For myself, I wouldn't
care for it.

VETA. Hear that, Judge! Hear that, Doctor! That's what we
have to put up with.

ELWOOD. (*Turning to look at her.*) Veta, do you want me to
take this?

VETA. Elwood, I'm only thinking of you. You're my brother
and I've known you for years. I'd do anything for you. That
Harvey wouldn't do anything for you. He's making a fool
out of you, Elwood. Don't be a fool.

ELWOOD. Oh, I won't.

VETA. Why, you could amount to something. You could be
sitting on the Western Slope Water Board right now if you'd
only go over and ask them.

ELWOOD. All right, Veta. If that's what you want, Harvey and
I will go over and ask them tomorrow.

VETA. Tomorrow! I never want to see another tomorrow. Not
if Myrtle Mae and I have to live in the house with that rabbit. Our friends never come to see us—we have no social
life; we have no life at all. We're both miserable. I wish I
were dead—but maybe you don't care!

ELWOOD. (*Slowly.*) I've always felt that Veta should have
everything she wants. Veta, are you sure? (VETA *nods.*) I'll
take it. Where do I go, Doctor?

CHUMLEY. In Dr. Sanderson's office, Dowd.

ELWOOD. Say goodbye to the old fellow for me, won't you?
(*Exits* U.L. CHUMLEY *exits* C.)

JUDGE. How long will this take, Doctor?

SANDERSON. Only a few minutes. Why don't you wait? (*Exits.*)

JUDGE. We'll wait. (*Sits* L. *of desk.*)

66

VETA. *(Sighs.)* Dr. Sanderson said it wouldn't take long.

MYRTLE. Now, Mother, don't fidget.

VETA. Oh, how can I help it?

MYRTLE. *(Picks up edge of draperies.)* How stunning! Mother, could you see me in a house-coat of this material?

VETA. *(To* MYRTLE—*first looking at draperies. Sighs again.)* Yes, dear, but let me get a good night's sleep first. *(Loud knocking at door.)*

JUDGE. Come in. *(Enter* CAB DRIVER.*)* What do you want?

CAB DRIVER. I'm lookin' for a little, short—*(Seeing* VETA.*)* Oh, there you are! Lady, you jumped outta the cab without payin' me.

VETA. Oh, yes. I forgot. How much is it?

CAB DRIVER. All the way out here from town? $2.75.

VETA. *(Looking in purse.)* $2.75! I could have sworn I brought my coin purse—where is it? *(Gets up, goes to table, turns pocketbook upside down, in full view of audience. Nothing comes out of it but a compact and a handerkerchief.)* Myrtle, do you have any money?

MYRTLE. I spent that money Uncle Elwood gave me for my new hair-do for the party.

VETA. Judge, do you have $2.75 I could give this man?

JUDGE. Sorry. Nothing but a check.

CAB DRIVER. We don't take checks.

JUDGE. I know.

VETA. Dr. Chumley, do you happen to have $2.75 I could borrow to pay this cab driver?

CHUMLEY. *(He has just entered* C., *now wearing white starched jacket.)* Haven't got my wallet. No time to get it now. Have to get on with this injection. Sorry. *(Exits* L.*)*

VETA. Well, I'll get it for you from my brother, but I can't get it right now. He's in there to get an injection. It won't be long. You'll have to wait.

CAB DRIVER. You're gonna get my money from your brother and he's in there to get some of that stuff they shoot out here?

VETA. Yes, it won't be but a few minutes.

CAB DRIVER. Lady, I want my money now.

VETA. But I told you it would only be a few minutes. I want you to drive us back to town, anyway.

CAB DRIVER. And I told you I want my money now or I'm nosin' the cab back to town, and you can wait for the bus—at six in the morning.

VETA. Well, of all the pig-headed, stubborn things—!

MYRTLE. I should say so.

JUDGE. What's the matter with you?

CAB DRIVER. Nothin' that $2.75 won't fix. You heard me. Take it or leave it.

VETA. (*Getting up, going* L.) I never heard of anything so unreasonable in my life. (*Knocks.*) Dr. Chumley, will you let Elwood step out here a minute. This cab driver won't wait.

CHUMLEY. (*Off* L.) Don't be too long. (*Enter* ELWOOD. CHUMLEY *follows.*)

VETA. Elwood, I came off without my coin purse. Will you give this man $2.75? But don't give him any more. He's been very rude.

ELWOOD. (*Extending his hand.*) How do you do? Dowd is my name. Elwood P.

CAB DRIVER. Lofgren's mine. E. J.

ELWOOD. I'm glad to meet you, Mr. Lofgren. This is my sister, Mrs. Simmons. My charming little niece, Myrtle Mae Simmons. Judge Gaffney and Dr. Chumley. (ALL *bow coldly.*)

CAB DRIVER. Hi—

ELWOOD. Have you lived around here long, Mr. Lofgren?

CAB DRIVER. Yeah, I've lived around here all my life.

ELWOOD. Do you enjoy your work?

CAB DRIVER. It's O.K. I been with the Apex Cabs fifteen years and my brother Joe's been drivin' for Brown Cabs pretty near twelve.

ELWOOD. You drive for Apex and your brother Joe for Brown's? That's interesting, isn't it, Veta? (VETA *reacts with a sniff.*) Mr. Lofgren—let me give you one of my cards. (*Gives him one.*)

CHUMLEY. Better get on with this, Mr. Dowd.

ELWOOD. Certainly. One minute. My sister and my charming little niece live here with me at this address. Won't you and your brother come and have dinner with us some time?

CABBY. Sure—be glad to.

ELWOOD. When—when would you be glad to?

CABBY. I couldn't come any night but Tuesday. I'm on duty all the rest of the week.

68

ELWOOD. You must come on Tuesday, then. We'll expect you and be delighted to see you, won't we, Veta?

VETA. Oh, Elwood, I'm sure this man has friends of his own.

ELWOOD. Veta, one can't have too many friends.

VETA. Elwood, don't keep Dr. Chumley waiting—that's rude.

ELWOOD. *Of course. (Gives him bill.)* Here you are—keep the change. I'm glad to have met you and I'll expect you Tuesday with your brother. Will you excuse me now?

LOFGREN. Sure. (ELWOOD *exits* U.L. CHUMLEY *follows.*)

CAB DRIVER. A sweet guy.

VETA. Certainly. You could just as well have waited.

CAB DRIVER. Oh, no. Listen, lady. I've been drivin' this route fifteen years. I've brought 'em out here to get that stuff and drove 'em back after they had it. It changes 'em. (*Crosses to desk.*)

VETA. Well, I certainly hope so.

CAB DRIVER. And you ain't kiddin'. On the way out here they sit back and enjoy the ride. They talk to me. Sometimes we stop and watch the sunsets and look at the birds flyin'. Sometimes we stop and watch the birds when there ain't no birds and look at the sunsets when it's rainin'. We have a swell time and I always get a big tip. But afterward—oh–oh —— (*Starts to exit again.*)

VETA. Afterwards—oh–oh! What do you mean afterwards—oh–oh?

CAB DRIVER. They crab, crab, crab. They yell at me to watch the lights, watch the brakes, watch the intersections. They scream at me to hurry. They got no faith—in me or my buggy—yet it's the same cab—the same driver—and we're goin' back over the very same road. It's no fun—and no tips— (*Turns to door.*)

VETA. But my brother would have tipped you, anyway. He's very generous. Always has been.

CAB DRIVER. Not after this he won't be. Lady, after this, he'll be a perfectly normal human being and you know what bastards they are! Glad I met you. I'll wait. (*Exits* L.)

VETA. (*Starts to run for door* U.L.) Oh, Judge Gaffney—Myrtle Mae! Stop it—stop it—don't give it to him! Elwood, come out of there.

JUDGE. You can't do that. Dr. Chumley is giving the injection.

69

MYRTLE. Mother—stop this ——

VETA. (*Pounding on door.*) I don't want Elwood to have it! I don't want Elwood that way. I don't like people like that.

MYRTLE. Do something with her, Judge—Mother, stop it ——

VETA. (*Turning on her.*) You shut up! I've lived longer than you have. I remember my father. I remember your father. I remember ——

CHUMLEY. (*Opens door.*) What's this? What's all this commotion?

WILSON. (*Enters* U.C.) What's the trouble, Doctor? She soundin' off again?

JUDGE. She wants to stop the injection.

VETA. You haven't—you haven't already given it to him, have you?

CHUMLEY. No, but we're ready. Take Mrs. Simmons away, Wilson.

VETA. Leave me alone. Take your hands off me, you white-slaver!

JUDGE. You don't know what you want. You didn't want that rabbit, either.

VETA. And what's wrong with Harvey? If Elwood and Myrtle Mae and I want to live with Harvey it's nothing to you! You don't even have to come around. It's our business. Elwood—Elwood! (ELWOOD *enters from* U.L. SHE *throws herself weepingly into his arms.* HE *pats her shoulder.*)

ELWOOD. There, there, Veta. (*To others.*) Veta is all tired out. She's done a lot today.

JUDGE. Have it your own way. I'm not giving up my game at the club again, not matter how big the animal is. (*He exits down* L.)

VETA. (*Crossing Elwood to desk.*) Come on, Elwood—let's get out of here. I hate this place. I wish I'd never seen it!

CHUMLEY. But—see—here——

ELWOOD. It's whatever Veta says, Doctor.

VETA. Why, look at this! That's funny. (*It's her coin purse.*) It must have been there all the time. I could have paid that cab driver myself. Harvey!

VETA. Come on, Myrtle Mae. Come on, Elwood. Hurry up. (*She exits down left.* MYRTLE *follows.*)

ELWOOD. Good night, Doctor Chumley. Good night, Mr.

Wilson.

VETA. (*Off stage.*) Come along Elwood.

ELWOOD. Doctor, for years I've known what my family thinks of Harvey. But I've often wondered what Harvey's family thinks of me. (*He looks beyond* CHUMLEY *to the door of his office* R.) Oh—there you are! Doctor—do you mind? (*Gestures for him to step back.*) You're standing in his way. (*There is the sound of a lock clicking open and the door of* CHUMLEY'S *office opens wide. The invisible Harvey crosses to him and as they exit together.*) Where've you been? I've been looking all over for you ——

CURTAIN

PROPERTIES

ACT I – SCENE I

2 Pictures in frames
Curtains and draperies
2 Roller Shades
Harvey hat and topcoat
Bunch roses
Smilax
Jardiniere with fern
Cut-glass bowl
Imitation books
Telephone
2 Gilt candlesticks
Pottery lamp and silk shade
Brass fender
2 Andirons

Set fire tools
Arm-chair red with velvet
Lamp and glass shade
2 Arm-chairs with red seats
Side chair with red seats
brocatelle
2 Side chairs with brown velvet
brocatelle
Carved living-room table
Melodion
Victorian stool, upholstered
2 Bookcases, one with books in it
Mantelpiece, with backing

ACT II – SCENE II

1 Butterfly table
1 Set encyclopedia
3 Windsor chairs
3 Side chairs with blue seats
1 Small filing case
1 Bookcase
1 Mantel clock
1 Office desk
Large medical books
Several assorted books
Inkstand
Humidor with cigars
Desk blotter
Drapery and small curtains

Bathrobe
1 Smoking stand
2 Tree branches
Window seat and pad
2 Telephones
1 Dressing-room chair
Wooden crates
9 shoes and covers
2 Lobby frames and 2 crates
1 Prop. box and contents
1 Bouquet of dahlias
1 Box of cards with "Elwood P. Dowd"

NEW PLAYS

★ **MOTHERS AND SONS by Terrence McNally.** At turns funny and powerful, MOTHERS AND SONS portrays a woman who pays an unexpected visit to the New York apartment of her late son's partner, who is now married to another man and has a young son. Challenged to face how society has changed around her, generations collide as she revisits the past and begins to see the life her son might have led. "A resonant elegy for a ravaged generation." –NY Times. "A moving reflection on a changed America." –Chicago Tribune. [2M, 1W, 1 boy] ISBN: 978-0-8222-3183-7

★ **THE HEIR APPARENT by David Ives, adapted from Le Légataire Universel by Jean-François Regnard.** Paris, 1708. Eraste, a worthy though penniless young man, is in love with the fair Isabelle, but her forbidding mother, Madame Argante, will only let the two marry if Eraste can show he will inherit the estate of his rich but miserly Uncle Geronte. Unfortunately, old Geronte has also fallen for the fair Isabelle, and plans to marry her this very day and leave her everything in his will—separating the two young lovers forever. Eraste's wily servant Crispin jumps in, getting a couple of meddling relatives disinherited by impersonating them (one, a brash American, the other a French female country cousin)—only to have the old man kick off before his will is made! In a brilliant stroke, Crispin then impersonates the old man, dictating a will favorable to his master (and Crispin himself, of course)—only to find that rich Uncle Geronte isn't dead at all and is more than ever ready to marry Isabelle! The multiple strands of the plot are unraveled to great comic effect in the streaming rhyming couplets of French classical comedy, and everyone lives happily, and richly, ever after. [4M, 3W] ISBN: 978-0-8222-2808-0

★ **HANDLE WITH CARE by Jason Odell Williams.** Circumstances both hilarious and tragic bring together a young Israeli woman, who has little command of English, and a young American man, who has little command of romance. Is their inevitable love an accident…or is it destiny, generations in the making? "A hilarious and heart-warming romantic comedy." –NY Times. "Hilariously funny! Utterly charming, fearlessly adorable and a tiny bit magical." –Naples News. [2M, 2W] ISBN: 978-0-8222-3138-7

★ **LAST GAS by John Cariani.** Nat Paradis is a Red Sox-loving part-time dad who manages Paradis' Last Convenient Store, the last convenient place to get gas—or anything—before the Canadian border to the north and the North Maine Woods to the west. When an old flame returns to town, Nat gets a chance to rekindle a romance he gave up on years ago. But sparks fly as he's forced to choose between new love and old. "Peppered with poignant characters [and] sharp writing." –Portland Phoenix. "Very funny and surprisingly thought-provoking." –Portland Press Herald. [4M, 3W] ISBN: 978-0-8222-3232-2

DRAMATISTS PLAY SERVICE, INC.
440 Park Avenue South, New York, NY 10016 212-683-8960 Fax 212-213-1539
postmaster@dramatists.com www.dramatists.com

NEW PLAYS

★ **ACT ONE by James Lapine.** Growing up in an impoverished Bronx family and forced to drop out of school at age thirteen, Moss Hart dreamed of joining the glamorous world of the theater. Hart's famous memoir *Act One* plots his unlikely collaboration with the legendary playwright George S. Kaufman and his arrival on Broadway. Tony Award-winning writer and director James Lapine has adapted Act One for the stage, creating a funny, heartbreaking and suspenseful celebration of a playwright and his work. "…brims contagiously with the ineffable, irrational and irrefutable passion for that endangered religion called the Theater." –NY Times. "…wrought with abundant skill and empathy." –Time Out. [8M, 4W] ISBN: 978-0-8222-3217-9

★ **THE VEIL by Conor McPherson.** May 1822, rural Ireland. The defrocked Reverend Berkeley arrives at the crumbling former glory of Mount Prospect House to accompany a young woman to England. Seventeen-year-old Hannah is to be married off to a marquis in order to resolve the debts of her mother's estate. However, compelled by the strange voices that haunt his beautiful young charge and a fascination with the psychic current that pervades the house, Berkeley proposes a séance, the consequences of which are catastrophic. "…an effective mixture of dark comedy and suspense." –Telegraph (London). "A cracking fireside tale of haunting and decay." –Times (London). [3M, 5W] ISBN: 978-0-8222-3313-8

★ **AN OCTOROON by Branden Jacobs-Jenkins. Winner of the 2014 OBIE Award for Best New American Play.** Judge Peyton is dead and his plantation Terrebonne is in financial ruins. Peyton's handsome nephew George arrives as heir apparent and quickly falls in love with Zoe, a beautiful octoroon. But the evil overseer M'Closky has other plans—for both Terrebonne and Zoe. In 1859, a famous Irishman wrote this play about slavery in America. Now an American tries to write his own. "AN OCTOROON invites us to laugh loudly and easily at how naïve the old stereotypes now seem, until nothing seems funny at all." –NY Times [10M, 5W] ISBN: 978-0-8222-3226-1

★ **IVANOV translated and adapted by Curt Columbus.** In this fascinating early work by Anton Chekhov, we see the union of humor and pathos that would become his trademark. A restless man, Nicholai Ivanov struggles to dig himself out of debt and out of provincial boredom. When the local doctor, Lvov, informs Ivanov that his wife Anna is dying and accuses him of worsening her condition with his foul moods, Ivanov is sent into a downward spiral of depression and ennui. He soon finds himself drawn to a beautiful young woman, Sasha, full of hope and energy. Finding himself stuck between a romantic young mistress and his ailing wife, Ivanov falls deeper into crisis, heading toward inevitable tragedy. [8M, 8W] ISBN: 978-0-8222-3155-4

DRAMATISTS PLAY SERVICE, INC.
440 Park Avenue South, New York, NY 10016 212-683-8960 Fax 212-213-1539
postmaster@dramatists.com www.dramatists.com

NEW PLAYS

★ **I'LL EAT YOU LAST: A CHAT WITH SUE MENGERS by John Logan.** For more than 20 years, Sue Mengers' clients were the biggest names in show business: Barbra Streisand, Faye Dunaway, Burt Reynolds, Ali MacGraw, Gene Hackman, Cher, Candice Bergen, Ryan O'Neal, Nick Nolte, Mike Nichols, Gore Vidal, Bob Fosse…If her clients were the talk of the town, she was the town, and her dinner parties were the envy of Hollywood. Now, you're invited into her glamorous Beverly Hills home for an evening of dish, dirty secrets and all the inside showbiz details only Sue can tell you. "A delectable soufflé of a solo show…thanks to the buoyant, witty writing of Mr. Logan" –NY Times. "80 irresistible minutes of primo tinseltown dish from a certified master chef." –Hollywood Reporter. [1W] ISBN: 978-0-8222-3079-3

★ **PUNK ROCK by Simon Stephens.** In a private school outside of Manchester, England, a group of highly-articulate seventeen-year-olds flirt and posture their way through the day while preparing for their A-Level mock exams. With hormones raging and minimal adult supervision, the students must prepare for their future — and survive the savagery of high school. Inspired by playwright Simon Stephens' own experiences as a teacher, PUNK ROCK is an honest and unnerving chronicle of contemporary adolescence. "[A] tender, ferocious and frightning play." –NY Times. "[A] muscular little play that starts out funny and ferocious then reveals its compassion by degrees." –Hollywood Reporter. [5M, 3W] ISBN: 978-0-8222-3288-9

★ **THE COUNTRY HOUSE by Donald Margulies.** A brood of famous and longing-to-be-famous creative artists have gathered at their summer home during the Williamstown Theatre Festival. When the weekend takes an unexpected turn, everyone is forced to improvise, inciting a series of simmering jealousies, romantic outbursts, and passionate soul-searching. Both witty and compelling, THE COUNTRY HOUSE provides a piercing look at a family of performers coming to terms with the roles they play in each other's lives. "A valentine to the artists of the stage." –NY Times. "Remarkably candid and funny." –Variety. [3M, 3W] ISBN: 978-0-8222-3274-2

★ **OUR LADY OF KIBEHO by Katori Hall.** Based on real events, OUR LADY OF KIBEHO is an exploration of faith, doubt, and the power and consequences of both. In 1981, a village girl in Rwanda claims to see the Virgin Mary. Ostracized by her schoolmates and labeled disturbed, everyone refuses to believe, until impossible happenings appear again and again. Skepticism gives way to fear, and then to belief, causing upheaval in the school community and beyond. "Transfixing." –NY Times. "Hall's passionate play renews belief in what theater can do." –Time Out [7M, 8W, 1 boy] ISBN: 978-0-8222-3301-5

DRAMATISTS PLAY SERVICE, INC.
440 Park Avenue South, New York, NY 10016 212-683-8960 Fax 212-213-1539
postmaster@dramatists.com www.dramatists.com

NEW PLAYS

★ **AGES OF THE MOON by Sam Shepard.** Byron and Ames are old friends, reunited by mutual desperation. Over bourbon on ice, they sit, reflect and bicker until fifty years of love, friendship and rivalry are put to the test at the barrel of a gun. "A poignant and honest continuation of themes that have always been present in the work of one of this country's most important dramatists, here reconsidered in the light and shadow of time passed." –NY Times. "Finely wrought…as enjoyable and enlightening as a night spent stargazing." –Talkin' Broadway. [2M] ISBN: 978-0-8222-2462-4

★ **ALL THE WAY by Robert Schenkkan. Winner of the 2014 Tony Award for Best Play.** November, 1963. An assassin's bullet catapults Lyndon Baines Johnson into the presidency. A Shakespearean figure of towering ambition and appetite, this charismatic, conflicted Texan hurls himself into the passage of the Civil Rights Act—a tinderbox issue emblematic of a divided America—even as he campaigns for re-election in his own right, and the recognition he so desperately wants. In Pulitzer Prize and Tony Award–winning Robert Schenkkan's vivid dramatization of LBJ's first year in office, means versus ends plays out on the precipice of modern America. ALL THE WAY is a searing, enthralling exploration of the morality of power. It's not personal, it's just politics. "…action-packed, thoroughly gripping… jaw-dropping political drama." –Variety. "A theatrical coup…nonstop action. The suspense of a first-class thriller." –NY1. [17M, 3W] ISBN: 978-0-8222-3181-3

★ **CHOIR BOY by Tarell Alvin McCraney.** The Charles R. Drew Prep School for Boys is dedicated to the creation of strong, ethical black men. Pharus wants nothing more than to take his rightful place as leader of the school's legendary gospel choir. Can he find his way inside the hallowed halls of this institution if he sings in his own key? "[An] affecting and honest portrait…of a gay youth tentatively beginning to find the courage to let the truth about himself become known." –NY Times. "In his stirring and stylishly told drama, Tarell Alvin McCraney cannily explores race and sexuality and the graces and gravity of history." –NY Daily News. [7M] ISBN: 978-0-8222-3116-5

★ **THE ELECTRIC BABY by Stefanie Zadravec.** When Helen causes a car accident that kills a young man, a group of fractured souls cross paths and connect around a mysterious dying baby who glows like the moon. Folk tales and folklore weave throughout this magical story of sad endings, strange beginnings and the unlikely people that get you from one place to the next. "The imperceptible magic that pervades human existence and the power of myth to assuage sorrow are invoked by the playwright as she entwines the lives of strangers in THE ELECTRIC BABY, a touching drama." –NY Times. "As dazzling as the dialogue is dreamful." –Pittsburgh City Paper. [3M, 3W] ISBN: 978-0-8222-3011-3

DRAMATISTS PLAY SERVICE, INC.
440 Park Avenue South, New York, NY 10016 212-683-8960 Fax 212-213-1539
postmaster@dramatists.com www.dramatists.com